THE TECHNIQUES OF GRAPHIC ART

THE TECHNIQUES OF GRAPHIC ART

by H. van Kruiningen

translated by B. K. Bowes

foreword by Jos de Gruyter

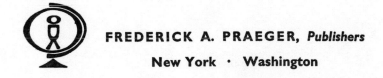

FREDERICK A. PRAEGER, *Publishers*

New York · Washington

BOOKS THAT MATTER
Published in the United States of America in 1969
by Frederick A. Praeger, Inc., Publishers
111 Fourth Avenue, New York, N.Y. 10003

This book was first published in 1966 in Dutch under the title *Techniek van de Grafische Kunst* by Lemniscaat, Rotterdam

Library of Congress Catalog Card Number: 74–83502

Printed in Great Britain

FOREWORD

ART is always an interplay between creativeness and use of material, or to put it another way, between creativeness and technique. This used to be expressed differently and more pretentiously; for example, people used to speak of a marriage between spirit and matter. But it all boils down to the same thing: the recognition that the materials an artist selects and the way in which he uses and controls them are of essential, if not decisive, importance, for the result. This surely suggests that some knowledge of materials and techniques will also make things clearer for those who look at works of art. Their understanding will be increased, and their enjoyment will be doubled.

Artistic comprehension does not drop from the skies. At best, we can enjoy a fugue by Bach or a symphony by Brahms without knowing anything about music. But how much richer our experience will be if we have learned to follow the polyphonic structure of a fugue or have some idea of the instrumental composition of an orchestra! If the same applies to a drawing or a painting, it is even more true in the case of graphic techniques, with their infinite possibilities. Woodcutting, etching and lithography (to confine ourselves to the well-known classification of relief, intaglio and surface printing) use quite different materials and offer the artist radically different opportunities of expression. The lumping of this rich variety together as the art of the print and the use of the title *The Techniques of Graphic Art* (note the use of the singular!) by van Kruiningen for his book are naturally highly significant. For drawings and paintings are unique, but any printing plate lends itself to multiplication and owes its origin to this. Graphic art was once used largely for illustrations or reproductions, for example for reproducing paintings before the invention of photography. In the twentieth century, however, it has acquired an independent character. The eminently democratic nature of graphic art, due to its capacity for multiplication, deserves to be stressed. This democratic character has come to the fore since the Second World War. Graphic art as a whole has evolved from the days when it was a fine art for connoisseurs, producing masterpieces that were put away in portfolios and taken out to be admired from time to time. Nowadays it gives us products of convenient size, which we like to frame and hang on the wall. The great revival of graphic art in the Netherlands, and as much, if not more, in other countries as well, is due to this. It has not become a "folk art", but an art for people in all walks of life. From a social point of view it fits perfectly in the framework of our times.

What I have just said may show how much I welcome the appearance of this book. I know from experience that many people really want to know how etchings, aquatints, lithographs, woodcuts or line-engravings are produced. The previous generation's reaction tended to be purely aesthetic, but nowadays people concentrate on "doing" or "do-it-yourself", on knowing why and how. Van Kruiningen is a good guide, because his keen, practical approach enables him to write both for the expert and the layman. He has been known for a long time as an important artist, and he is also known as a committed and versatile craftsman with a delightful flair for experimenting. He has no bees in his bonnet and keeps a completely open mind. I have myself practised most of the techniques he describes as a pupil of the Royal College of Art in London, and so I can vouch for the correctness and clarity of his descriptions. He is also interested in the past, which need not surprise us in an artist who has more than once chosen ancient myths as material for his prints. The brief historical introductions put the expositions of this craft in a perspective that is full of suggestion.

JOS DE GRUYTER

CONTENTS

WHAT IS GRAPHIC ART?

THE word "graphic" is derived from the Greek word meaning "to write". But new developments often give additional meanings to old, naturalized names, and this word has added "printing" to its original meaning.

For "graphic art" means the art that can be reproduced by hand by printing techniques. All kinds of methods may be used. We can print off wood, linoleum, metal and stone, and sometimes off silk or some other material; in the latter cases the term "silk-screen printing" is used. When we are talking about graphic art, we call the product of one of these materials a "print". Now the term "print" is an elastic one. The first printed image was made from a simple engraved wooden or bone block on parchment or cloth some three or four thousand years ago. These can hardly be called prints; nevertheless, these primitive products are the beginning of the story. We have found dozens of these small stamps. Few of them have been made of wood, because this has decayed in the course of centuries, but many specimens fashioned of bone, metal and baked or dried clay have been discovered. These stamps provided the first form of relief printing.

RELIEF PRINTING

"RELIEF printing" is the name we give to the method in which the ink is in relief, as may be seen clearly in the case of woodcuts. Everything that is to remain white is cut away from a block of wood. When we deposit ink with rollers on the parts that have not been cut away the ink is in relief, hence the name "relief printing". This was the first method to be used in graphic art. The stamps were not only used by the Chinese, but also were known to the Greeks and Romans. Emperors, kings and merchants went about with these stamps, often attached to a piece of string round the neck, for stamping contracts to purchase, charters, etc.

We know that large editions were printed at an early date. In Japan, an edition of more than one million was printed in 770 from wooden, metal and porcelain blocks. But the Chinese were much earlier in the field; they started printing in the second century A.D. They did this shortly after the Chinese Minister Ts'ai Lun told the emperor in the year 105 about a new method for manufacturing paper; a kind of paper had already been made from pulped silk.

Hemp, bark and rags were used for this new method of making paper. A fine pulp was prepared from these materials, and the paper was produced with a frame on which wires were stretched. Once this paper had been made, people wanted to use it, but not yet for printing; all kinds of things were made of it, such as clothes, caps and Chinese lanterns. In about the year 150, the Chinese began to produce peculiar copies of existing reliefs. Later on, special stones were made for this method, which we now call "rubbing". It has nothing to do with lithography, which is also a kind of stone printing; it is a combination of relief and intaglio printing, which we shall be dealing with later. In the fifth century editions were already being printed for school-books. It is also known that playing-cards were made in this way.

The Chinese had large libraries at a very early date. Buddhist and Taoist books were copied again and again by scribes. To preserve the authenticity of the works, one of the emperors had them all engraved on stone in 837. The emperor might have been expected to have the works printed from the stone, but he did not do so. Shortly afterwards the characters of the text were cut on 130,000 wooden blocks. The wooden blocks were not printed on presses, but manually sheet by sheet. The Chinese did not restrict themselves to the text; loose prints showing figures of the Buddha are also preserved. A very attractive woodcut dating from the time of "primitive" Chinese woodcutting has been preserved entire.

In 1901 the Chinese monk Wang made an important discovery. While searching for remains of old frescoes, he found a hole behind some fresco in a cellar of an old, abandoned Buddhist monastery in one of the offshoots of the Great Wall of China. He crept in and discovered a room in which lay a large number of linen-wrapped packages. Each package was found to contain twelve rolls. The monk closed the hole again and endeavoured to keep his discovery secret. But one or two years later he confided in a few Western scholars. They discovered 15,000 rolls, written by hand except for four books, which were printed. One of these contained the *Diamond Sutra*. It was dated 11th May 868, and is the first dated printed book that has been discovered. It begins with an exceptionally beautiful woodcut measuring 35 x 28 cm

Acharius
abbas de/
scendit de
syti a intuit dormire
in monumento vbi
sepulta erant corpa
paganox a extraxit
vnu corp? fb caput
suu tanq pulmariu
Demones aut volé/
tes eu terré vocabát
qfi vnam mulierem
dicentes· surge veni
nobiscu ad balneuz
a aft demon sub ipo
tanq· ex mortuo illo
dicebat peregrinum
quendã habeo sup me et nõ possu venire.Ille aut nõ expauit
fz rñdebat corp? illud dicens surge a vade si potes. a audiétes

Fifteenth-century book illustration (woodcut)

Block-book, fifteenth century

Woodcut, ninth century (China)

Wood-engraving, engraved in end-grain pear wood with the burin

Printing a woodcut

(14 x 11 in.). The scholars found fifty-four other woodcuts in the same cellar of this abandoned monastery. Some of them were bound together in small editions. The room had been closed for nine hundred years and had never been plundered.

The Chinese art of printing probably reached the West by the endless caravan routes, together with paper, bales of silk, etc. One of the first dated woodcuts in the West, representing Saint Christopher and bearing the year 1423, betrays very marked Chinese influence in its composition. The art of woodcutting began to develop in Western Europe in about 1400. Before 1400, woodcuts were usually printed on cloth. They were made for many purposes. They were stuck on boxes and doors; small prints were also stuck in prayer books; they were used for calendars and caricatures, and as talismans; they were sewn into coats or stuck in money-boxes. Before the invention of movable type, block-books containing dozens of prints were cut.

The first woodcuts tell us about trade, navigation, folklore, etc. They were produced on a large scale, being made and disseminated by several dozen monasteries in Western Europe. A bound collection, usually with a text printed at the side or underneath, soon formed the first book of prints. Movable type did not exist before 1450, and so the whole page was cut from a single block of wood, usually with some woodcuts for illustration. In these block-books, the pages were only printed on one side, and two of these pages were then stuck back to back. This is how books printed on both sides came into being.

Known block-books are the *Biblia Pauperum* ("The Bible of the Poor"), *Ars Moriendi* ("The Art of Dying"), *The Book of the Seven Planets* and many others. After the invention of printing, dozens of years passed by before we can really speak of production. The first books were not printed very clearly; the art was still in its infancy. The first editions before 1500 are therefore called *incunabula*, from the Latin word for a cradle. In 1480 the publisher Leeu te Gouda brought out *Dialogus Creaturarum*

Moralisatus; this book contained 121 very handsome woodcuts by an unknown artist. A very famous printer, draughtsman and woodcutter was Golard Mansion, who published twenty books before 1485, including Ovid's *Metamorphoses*. Mansion produced many woodcuts after miniatures. In the beginning these miniatures were not cut in mirror image, which was evidently found to be rather troublesome, but it did not take long before people also began to cut the miniatures in mirror image. Besides book illustrations and religious prints, many playing-cards were cut and printed in large quantities, since card games were very popular. A kind of manual entitled *Wooden Blocks for Playing Cards and Saints* appeared in Italy in 1430. Woodcutting was widely practised in the following centuries, although most of these woodcuts are reproductions of drawings.

Woodcuts and linocuts

Wood, knives and gouges

Practically any kind of wood can be used for making a woodcut. It depends how we go to work. Some artists cut with very fine knives, while others use cobblers' knives. Timber is least suitable. But even this may sometimes be used because of its coarse grain. Oak and similar woods are also good. The fine grain will often produce a special effect in the woodcut. To enhance this effect, the grain may be made somewhat deeper with a fine steel brush. Anyone who wishes to take advantage of this grain effect may also use the many kinds of veneer. Three-ply wood is sometimes suitable, although sharp knives must be used, or the veneer layer will soon splinter. But apple or pear is best for anyone who just wants to rely on a clean black-and-white effect. Old, worked wood is always better than new, which will be warped by atmospheric conditions. We often find very suitable specimens lining old cupboards. Plank wood, that is wood running with the grain and sawn into planks, can be worked with knives and gouges. In the Netherlands, pear is nearly always imported from France; the trees are thicker there, and the wood is of better quality.

Good results can be achieved with linoleum, as many artists have shown. In the view of the author, however, wood is preferable because of its natural resistance. It is a living material, harder and more rugged than linoleum. As we have just said, wood, unlike linoleum, offers some resistance, which must be overcome by the artist. This distinctive property results in a much more attractive cut, which is more pithy, more striking and even rather more uneven. This gives us something that is usually lacking in linocuts, unless an attempt is made to imitate this property in linoleum, as is sometimes done fairly successfully.

The gouges that we buy in shops cannot generally be used straight away. Any carpenter will also sharpen the tool that he has just bought. The front, sharpened part of the newly purchased gouge is too short and must have a longer slope. We must also grind the back of the gouge, which has to slide through the wood, until it is quite smooth. If we sharpen the gouge on a grindstone, we must be extremely careful; the thin front edge of the gouge soon shows black spots, a sign that the steel is burned and will later crumble very quickly. It is therefore best to use an emery stone or fine emery paper. A burr sometimes forms on the inside when sharpening; this can be best removed with the shaft of a paint brush with a piece of polishing paper wrapped round it.

Wood-engraving

Woodcuts went out in the eighteenth century, when drawings and paintings were reproduced by line-engravings and mezzotints. They could not compete in fineness with these intaglio techniques. The invention of wood-engraving changed this.

In about 1800, Thomas Bewick wished to compete with line-engraving by engraving on wood. To cut the gossamer lines in wood like line-engravers, he had to use a burin. But a burin cannot be used to cut plank wood; the direction of the grain frays the grooves. The burin is a steel pen of rectangular cross-section, the front end of which is ground obliquely, producing a razor-sharp lozenge shape. Wood and line-engravers sharpen their burins themselves, giving them the shape they desire. Finely sharpened chasers may also be used. Thomas Bewick hit on the idea of using end-grain blocks. The wood is cross-sawn into round pieces like slices of sausage. These are sawn into rectangular blocks, which are then glued together, but in a different order. The resulting planks are scoured and polished, practically always to letter height. Pear wood is an excellent material, but end-grain blocks of certain palm trees are still better, although much more expensive. When a wood-engraving is being cut, the block usually rests on a sandbag, like the one used by the line-engraver, or on a small wooden turntable. Good sharp burins are a first requirement. When sharpening a burin, the angle to which the facet is sharpened is important. An ingenious instrument has therefore been brought on to the market with which the burin and also chisels can be fixed in a certain position; the burin moves to and fro along the sharpening stone.

Printing the woodcut

Printer's ink is best for woodcuts and linocuts. To accelerate drying we may add some drying agent to the ink, but only a very little, otherwise the print will be shiny when it has dried. Some people mix powder with the ink to reduce shininess (for example, finely ground mica). For colour prints we can also use magnesium powder, not for mixing with the ink, but for spreading over the printed ink before it is dry. This results in rather a dull effect. It is better to pass the print between unprinted newspaper with a piece of felt through an etching press or mangle. Or simply to print by hand; this gives the best results. A wooden rolling-pin is excellent provided that the board underneath is level. Many woodcutters use a paper-knife or a spoon. Break the handle off a tablespoon and you have a splendid printing press. A press is quicker, but hard, cold, unfeeling woodcuts are often produced.

We achieve the best result by not printing too greasily and not wet on wet; let the print dry first before another colour is added. If we wish for any reason to print one after another, it is best to lay a sheet of unprinted newspaper over the still fresh print and rub it with the hand; the print should then be rubbed carefully with a rag and some magnesium powder; a new colour can now be printed on top. At first the layer of magnesium powder, which must be very thin, makes the print rather grey, but this disappears after a while.

The great difficulty is to put the colours over and next to each other just as we wish. This can sometimes be done with a little adjustment, but exact results will not be achieved by trusting to luck. We must be systematic. The blocks for each colour must be the same size. When we have made a design, we decide first whether the colours are to be printed adjacent to each other, or overlap in some places. In the latter case the number of colours will be much greater. By printing yellow over blue, for example, we get a greenish hue as well as yellow and blue. This can be done with other combinations, greatly increasing the possibilities. We usually start with the lightest colours. We place the first block in the middle of a drawing-board or sheet of cardboard and draw a line round it. Since all the colour blocks are the same size they fit exactly in this rectangle. If we now draw a line, for example 10 cm above it, and decide on a point where we wish to place the corner of the paper, and if we keep to this line and this corner point, each colour will come in the correct place. We can improve this method by sawing out the shape of the blocks, so that they fit in the resulting space. The paper will then, of course, be laid still more satisfactorily. If this operation is found to be very troublesome, the paper may be placed first on a stout sheet of cardboard, from which it projects 1 or 2 cm (approximately $\frac{1}{2}$ in to 1 in) so that it can be pushed on to the register line or against a strip of cardboard that has been stuck on there. Hold the paper firm with one hand and pull the cardboard away from underneath with the other; a little skill is needed, but this applies to graphic techniques in general. We may also use two pins, which are first pushed through four or five superimposed sheets of paper. During printing, the pins must fit exactly in the holes they have made.

The best paper to use is probably Japanese tissue paper, but the very thin rice paper is also excellent. Many other kinds may be used; but they must not contain wood, or they will yellow very quickly. Strawboard must never be attached behind a print, whether it is a woodcut, etching or lithograph. This is because strawboard contains acid, which is bound to get into the print after a time and turn it yellow.

INTAGLIO PRINTING

Origins and past techniques

INTAGLIO printing originated with the goldsmiths, and they or their sons were the engravers of the beginning of the fifteenth century. We have a print by the famous engraver Martin Schöngauer representing two goldsmith's boys. Albrecht Dürer's father followed this calling. Wishing to adorn the objects they made, such as weapons, armour, vases and dishes, the goldsmiths engraved all kinds of patterns in these copper, gold or silver articles with burins, steel pens whose tips had been sharpened to form forward-sloping, lozenge-shaped facets. They were able to make beautiful ornamentations with these burins at an early date. To show them up better, they filled the engraved lines with various substances, usually black ink or a kind of enamel, known as niello. They sometimes printed these designs, not for use as prints in their own right, but to preserve them for future clients or for pupils to use. The prints were also sold or given away to calligraphers, glaziers, carpet-weavers, etc., for them to copy. The first extant dated engraving is from 1446 and represents a goldsmith's workshop. This proves how closely the first engravers were connected with the craft of the goldsmith.

It was not at first the custom to sign prints; this was not done on a wide scale until the nineteenth century. As a result we do not know who made all those prints in the early days of the engraver's art. But to create some order in this multiplicity of unsigned prints, art historians have given names to the unknown artists. They may be named after the place where they worked and lived, or after a mysterious sign engraved on his plate by the engraver. For example, The Master W with the Key always put a W with a small key on his prints. Many "masters" engraved initials on their prints.

There was a halfway house between relief and intaglio printing—engraving in white on a stippled background. It is by no means accidental that this technique came into being in the transitional period between woodcutting and engraving. Individual artists started to print engravings like woodcuts. But these engravings were made specially for the purpose. It is more difficult to cut metal than wood, so that they were harder to produce than woodcuts. The copper was worked with knives and burins, but steel pens were also used for punching little holes, sometimes dozens of them close to each other, the burrs being scraped away carefully. When the plate was ready, it was inked with a dabber or roller; only the raised portions were coated with black ink, as in the case of woodcuts. A number of specimens have been preserved. But this process was soon abandoned; it was more complicated, more difficult and more expensive than woodcutting. Most of the extant prints have as a mark a shield with a heart and a Gothic "d". They were produced in about 1445, and constitute an interesting interlude in the infancy of graphic arts.

The goldsmiths did not only engrave on their products; some of them also etched all kinds of designs with "strong water", a nitric acid solution. These were often printed for the "archives" of the master, but an independent art of making prints did not yet exist.

We do not know who was the first to etch with the object of making a print. We have etchings by Dürer dating from 1515, and his fellow countryman Urs Graf was even earlier; the golden age came much later. For the time being, engraving was the main technique, even for reproducing paintings. Mass production of engravings soon developed. An important figure was the infant prodigy Lucas van Leyden. At the age of fourteen he reigned virtually supreme, and although he died fairly young, when only thirty-nine years old, he left behind him nearly two hundred prints. Engraving continued on a large scale in the following centuries; the engravers became more and more clever, and some tried to win a place apart by technical means.

In France, Callot and Nanteuil were the most famous engravers in the seventeenth century. Abraham Bosse also worked there. He wrote a textbook on etching. Bosse considered that the engraved line was much more attractive than the etched one, which he regarded as a cheap imitation. But he recognized that etching was much quicker and less laborious. He therefore devised an entirely new process retaining the character of the engraved line. This begins with a point and then becomes broader, because the burin cuts into the metal, but ends in a point again when the burin leaves the metal. Bosse's task was therefore not so easy. He developed an entirely new etching needle, which he called the "échoppe". This is a thin, round steel needle whose point is cut off obliquely; the point becomes broader towards the top. By starting with the point in the wax and then slowly turning the needle so that the point becomes broader and a greater breadth of the ground is also removed, a line is produced that bears a deceptive resemblance to an engraved one. This line is subsequently bitten in the acid bath. With a great deal of practice we can produce lines bitten in the metal at very regular intervals, so that even experts find it hard to tell the difference. But careful examination will reveal it. An engraved line is faultlessly neat because of the way of working, while an etched line is never so sound and smooth. The acid certainly does not help to produce this property of the engraved line. Moreover, the engraver drives more firmly into the metal with the burin than with the *échoppe*, which must be turned constantly when sliding over the copper through the layer of varnish. For this, we need to be something of a juggler.

Such a man was Claude Mellan, who lived at the same time as Bosse. He not only succeeded in imitating engraving with parallel lines, which did not cross each other at any point, but also managed, like a graphic acrobat, to make etchings that must have been admired by many people in those days. His *Napkin of Saint Veronica* is etched from a single line, hundreds of yards long, starting at the tip of the nose.

Engraving had its ups and downs as it developed through the centuries. It has been practised until our own times, and its adoption by young, modern grahpic artists shows that there is no need to turn up our noses at apparently out-of-date techniques. For whichever one an artist uses, the important point is, has he something to communicate? If so, all techniques are suitable, and none are inferior. With a good work of art you must be able to forget the technique, and any process is permitted if it benefits the power of expression.

In about the year 1640 Ludwig von Siegen, a German living in Utrecht, employed a new technique, "mezzotint". This process, which will be dealt with later, was very widely used for reproducing paintings, not only in black and white, but also in colour. Von Siegen made a number of fine mezzotints. A. Blooteling perfected the method by the use of the rocker. Vaillant, a Frenchman who worked a great deal in the Netherlands, also used mainly this technique. The mezzotint soon crossed over to England, where it was greatly used for the art of portraiture. It was also excellent for the reproduction of paintings. In our time mezzotints are not produced very often; they were still made recently in the Netherlands by M. C. Escher.

Intaglio printing was often practised in the Netherlands in the seventeenth century. The technique was very popular with painters, and when they had discovered etching practically everyone practised it. Rembrandt and Hercules Seghers are the greatest etchers of the seventeenth century in the Netherlands. There is no room in this book for a detailed discussion of Rembrandt's etchings, but something may be said about his technique and particularly about that of Hercules Seghers. One of the first etchings made by Rembrandt, a self-portrait, has a special feature. He probably drew in the etching layer with a split goose-quill or a two-pointed etching needle, since many of the lines are double; but we do not find this in any of his later etchings. Rembrandt was very probably on friendly terms with Hercules Seghers, who was sixteen years older; the latter used a variety of methods that had not been tried out before. He was quite misunderstood in his own time. Some years after his death Van Hoogstraten wrote, "The plate-printers took his prints in basketfuls to the grocers for packing butter and soap in and for use as cornets." In all, sixty etchings by Seghers are known, but he may well have made more, perhaps many more. It is difficult to see from his work how it was produced.

Goya used aquatint in many prints. Many etchings were made in the eighteenth and nineteenth centuries, but not many new methods were added to those already in existence. Iron plates were sometimes used. Albrecht Dürer made five etchings on iron plates, including his well-known print "The Cannon". But iron has no advantage over copper or zinc.

Materials

Only a few materials are used for intaglio printing. In practice we are confined to copper and zinc; silver, iron, tin or plastics may be employed exceptionally, but copper and zinc have always been the most favoured. Copper plates of 1 to $1\frac{1}{2}$ mm are probably the choicest material; they may be red or yellow; for our purpose red is best.

A lot of work is also done on zinc, which is softer and also gives us a different bitten line. Acid attacks zinc more unevenly than copper. Comparison between a printed line from a copper plate and one from a zinc plate does not reveal very much difference, but with hundreds of lines it is quite a different story. This need not be to the disadvantage of zinc. It all depends what is wanted, what the appearance of an etching is to be. A line bitten in zinc is rather more granular at the edges and therefore has a charm of its own. The difference is not very great, and much depends on the acid bath. Zinc is much cheaper than copper. It is claimed that a tone will appear between the lines much more quickly with zinc printing. This may happen, but a zinc plate can be polished well enough to produce a clean white copy. We shall return to this point when dealing with the printing of the plate.

Many more prints can be made from copper. Another advantage of copper is that we can face it with steel. If a large edition is to be printed, it is advisable to steel-face the copper and not wait until it deteriorates noticeably, which happens fairly quickly, for example with very fine parts. The layer of steel is so thin that it is invisible; it does not have the slightest effect on the copy and makes a practically unlimited edition possible. Zinc can also be steel-faced, but this is much more difficult and the chance of failure is greater. People are therefore less ready to try it.

Dry-point

Dry-point is the simplest of all intaglio-printing techniques. It may be practised on copper, zinc or tin. The plate is scratched with a sharp steel needle. The difference between a line produced by dry-point and an etched line will be seen immediately; an etched line nearly always has a blunt beginning and end; a line produced by dry-point has a pointed beginning and end. But the greatest difference is probably the burr. Burrs are produced by

Line-engraving *Ecce Homo* by Lucas van Leyden, 1510 (28·5 × 45 cm; 11·2 × 17·7 in)

Line-engraving; the engraver
at work

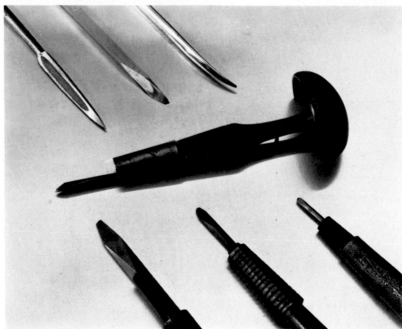

The line-engraver's tools
(burins, scraper and
burnisher)

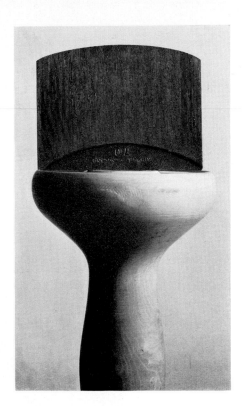

The rocker

The plate is given the burr with the rocker

pressing the needle hard on to the metal and pulling the needle towards oneself. A curl of metal is not formed as with engraving, but a milled, raised edge all along the line. The deeper and harder we dig the coarser the burr will be.

By scratching the metal gently with a sharp needle we can produce fine grey tones, over which thick lines may be drawn. The plate must generally be smoother before we begin, and therefore more polished, than an etching plate. The latter can be polished after etching, but this is not so easy with a dry-point plate if we do not wish to damage the burr.

The printing of a dry-point plate is practically the same as that of an etching or engraving. With dry-point, both the scratched line and the burr hold the ink. That is the object of this technique; the printed line has a frayed, somewhat outflowing line. The deep-black, velvety parts can be printed by making a large number of scratches beside and over each other. Copper is naturally best for dry-point; the burr forming on the edges of the lines is harder, and the copper can be steel-faced.

The number of prints that can be made cannot be stated definitely, but if we take a normally bitten plate with a not too fine aquatint, then we can make 150 to 200 prints or more from a copper plate, 50 to 75 from zinc and 4 or 5 or sometimes 10 to 15 with dry-point. The first two or three are always the best; when the first print is made, the burr is somewhat flattened. Burrs on copper plates will keep their shape better. The author has made 25 good prints from a copper plate by the dry-point process.

A new piece of tin is most suitable for anyone who cannot or does not wish to use copper or zinc. The burr is as hard as steel. Very beautiful prints can be made from tin plates, but the hardness of this metal means that it must be pressed and scratched much harder with the needle. A tin plate must be cleaned very well after printing and put in wax, because this metal corrodes rapidly. It is quite easy to wipe the ink off a smooth tin plate.

Dry-point is very old; "The Master of the Amsterdam Cabinet" made a large number of these prints in about 1450. Rembrandt also used the process a great deal for his etchings, thus creating a combined technique. We find this more frequently with Rembrandt than with his contemporaries. The cause was certainly not impatience over the preparation of the plate, but rather that he found the dry-point line with its rather outflowing, frayed deep-black tone more picturesque than the drier etched line. In his great etching *The Three Crosses* he probably reached the summit of his achievement in this field. The sight of the first or the fourth state is sure to make us think that he used another etching plate, since nothing is in the same place. He must have scraped away very large areas with a scraper and immediately scratched the figures in the copper again with a steel needle. Only if we try to see the old lines in some parts on the following print with the aid of a magnifying glass do we convince ourselves that Rembrandt certainly used one plate for this, perhaps the most beautiful of all his prints, and made a print whose plate had not lain in an etching bath. *The Three Crosses* is therefore not an etching, but a dry-point print.

Line-engraving

It is not so very difficult for anyone who can draw to make a dry-point plate or an etching. An engraving is quite a different story. Anyone who wishes to be anything like a master of the technique must first practise intensively for some years. A very firm hand is needed. The engraver does not scratch the metal, but digs into the plate with a paring chisel. He nearly always uses red copper, which is harder than zinc and gives a sounder line. The tool he uses is a burin, a rectangular steel pen which is ground to a V-shape at the front edge and mounted in a wooden handle.

The line-engraver sharpens his own burins; he knows exactly

how they fit the hand. Moreover, he does not possess only one or two, but several dozen, all of which have their own facets. The sharpening of all these burins is an art in itself. A special instrument is made for this purpose.

The very smooth polished plate is placed on a leather sand-bag. The engraver turns the plate on this bag while he digs the burin into the copper. Hardly any burr is formed, as with dry-point, but a curl of copper, which comes out of the line. The very fine burr that results is removed with a scraper. The engraved line starts with a point, then widens, and ends in another point. As the copper plate is polished until it is as smooth as a mirror, a tone is not produced on printing, but a clean black line on white paper.

The engraver's kit consists mainly of a number of burins, the leather sandbag, a scraper and burnisher, an adjustable instrument for holding the burins when sharpening, and a small chasing hammer for tapping out pits in the plate. These pits may occur if a large correction is made, when deep lines are abraded with the scraper.

Before worked copper plates were steel-faced, steel plates were also engraved.

Mezzotint

Mezzotint is not used very much nowadays. Hundreds of paintings were reproduced by this technique in the eighteenth and nineteenth centuries. Some of the reproductions were in colour; several plates were then used, but several colours were also applied to a single plate.

The inventor used in about 1640, when making the burr, a kind of roulette wheel, a turning ball in a handle. The ball had steel points on it. The artist starts with a surface as black as soot, on which, with infinite patience, he produces all tones of grey with his scraper and burnisher. The mezzotint process is based on an improvement of this system. Another dodge was used by Ludwig von Siegen, a German who lived in Utrecht. He might well be said to have been fascinated by the burr. When we dig a steel needle into a metal plate, we produce a sort of crater with a raised rim having sharp, angular edges; this is the "burr". Put a whole mass of these little pits close to each other, and you get a burr field. A rocker is used for this technique; this tool is in the form of a rather round chisel with a large number of sharp points (see illustration). If this area is inked and wiped clean again with muslin, a great deal of ink will remain between the burrs and therefore on the plate. This results in a fairly dark area on the print. If the burrs are pressed back with a smooth steel object and this is done so vigorously that the metal is kneaded smooth again on the area in question, we have then made a light area locally in the dark area.

Preparation of the copper or zinc plate

Copper or zinc plates may be polished or unpolished. At one time an artist would never have contemplated using an unpolished plate, but many prefer this nowadays. Later, on printing, a characteristic tone is obtained, which can also be produced by treating the plate with abrasive powder. If we want a mirror-smooth plate it must be polished. We can buy polished zinc and copper plates, and there are also polishers who will treat our plates for us. If we wish to do it ourselves, then we must start by buying a plate that is as sound as possible. A plumber or a good ironmonger will cut it for us to any size we require. If a number of etchings are to made, then it is much better to go to the wholesaler and buy a plate measuring 1 metre by 2 (3 ft 3 in by 6 ft 6 in), which may cut into different strips. The desired dimensions can be cut along an iron rule with a steel pen having a rather angular point. The edges of the plate are razor-sharp, and so they must be filed, especially at the sharp points. If the plate is 1·5 or 2 mm thick then a facet must be ground on the plate; otherwise the edge of the plate might cut into the blanket later when printing. An etching plate of 0·8 or 1 mm is usually thick enough.

Polishing and preparation of the plate

If we want to polish the plate we look for one that has as few scratches as possible. If there are one or two small scratches then we must carefully make the surface smooth with the burnisher; deeper scratches must first be mostly scraped away with the scraper and then treated with the burnisher. The plate should be rubbed as smooth as possible with abrasive powder, water and a soft flannel tag; we must press fairly hard at the beginning or we will not remove enough from the plate. The fine abrasive powder is made finer and finer by rubbing; in the end, it cannot be called abrasive powder any more, but the plate becomes smoother and smoother. A felt roller may also be used for polishing. Take a strip of felt about 12 cm (5 in) long, roll it up tight, tie it firmly with string, and you have a polishing felt that will last for years. But remember that one grain of sand or piece of zinc filing may spoil everything. After rinsing and drying, treat the plate with fine polishing paper, and finally with a copper polish. The plate is now like a mirror. Of course, all this will be done much more quickly with a lapping wheel run by a motor. You can also buy polishing pencils made of fine glass fibre, which, with a few drops of oil, may be used for local polishing.

If we scratch one of these smooth-polished plates with a sharp steel needle we may expect a beautiful, sound print with the dry-point technique, and a well-polished copper plate is also excellent material for the line-engraver. But the plate is less suitable for etching; the ground cannot "strike root", or adhere firmly enough, to the smooth surface.

Degreasing

If the ground is to adhere well to the plate the latter must not be polished too smoothly, and it must be completely free from grease. This can be achieved by making a paste of chalk and water to which a few drops of nitric acid are added; this is allowed to act on the plate for a moment. We may also plunge the plate for a moment in a weak acid solution, or hold it 1 or 2 centimetres (half an inch to an inch) above the acid bath for one or two hours. In that case, we take a sheet of cardboard that amply fits on the etching bath and cut a hole in it, which is 1 cm (0·4 in) smaller than the etching plate on both sides. The resulting microscopic holes are enough to make the etching ground adhere well. To see whether the plate is really free from grease we hold it under the tap; if the water draws away here and there there is still some greasiness, but if it runs off perfectly evenly then everything is as it should be.

Solid and liquid grounds

Before laying the ground we must make it or buy it ready-made. There are some very good ones on the market. Grounds are made of black balls of beeswax, resin, pitch and asphalt melted together in certain proportions.

An etcher will probably want to make his own ground, and the writer advises anyone taking up etching to do so. This will bring you in touch with the technical side of the craft, there is an attraction in doing things for yourself, and it will give you a better idea of the materials used. What is more, it is cheaper. Beeswax is the main component. Imitation beeswax may be purchased, but it is inadequate. Genuine beeswax smells sweet; it is sold in flakes and in lumps. A ground made of beeswax alone is much too soft; some resin and asphalt must be mixed with it, and the whole must be melted together well. There are many recipes for grounds, with small differences on the proportions, but they are all essentially the same. Here is an example of a composition:

2 parts by weight of beeswax,
1 part by weight of mastic,
1 part by weight of asphalt,
$\frac{1}{4}$ part by weight of Burgundy pitch.
or:
$2\frac{1}{2}$ parts by weight of beeswax,
$1\frac{1}{2}$ parts by weight of mastic,
$1\frac{1}{2}$ parts by weight of asphalt.

Mastic and Burgundy pitch are resins, which are bought in small lumps. Asphalt is obtainable in lumps and in powder form; the powder form is the best and may also be used for the aquatint techniques. First we melt the mastic, asphalt and Burgundy pitch together. All these substances are highly inflammable, and so caution is essential. The beeswax is added last. The mixture should be stirred up thoroughly for a few minutes with a stick. We pour this paste in stages into a vessel of lukewarm water. After a minute this stiffening paste will have become cool enough to be kneaded into balls. The balls must be kept free from dust; indeed the whole operation must be carried out with as little dust as possible. Beeswax may be bought from any chemist, lumps of mastic in a shop for graphic requisites, and asphalt or powder from a wholesaler of the graphic industry; alternatively, the chemist may be asked to order it from the wholesaler. Burgundy pitch is difficult to obtain, evidently being used only by etchers. It does not matter very much if this resin is not included.

Liquid ground, like the solid variety, may be bought ready-made. There are different types on the market. Le Frank's *Vernis à Couvrir* is good, and there are also some good British brands.

But we can also make the liquid ground ourselves; the simplest way is to dissolve a ball of solid ground that we have made ourselves with half turpentine, half turpentine substitute, as follows:

1 part by weight of solid ground, and
4 parts by weight of turpentine and turpentine substitute.

Turpentine substitute alone is satisfactory and results in quicker drying. Dust is even more undesirable with liquid than with solid ground. We should therefore take a funnel and strain the still warm liquid ground through a rag, so that the ground is free from dust when it enters the bottle. If we put some of this liquid in a saucer when using it, we must not pour what is left back into the bottle; this would introduce dust. These left-overs should be poured into another bottle for straining later on. The liquid ground may be used to cover the whole plate; it is also suitable for stopping-out parts and for retouching, although a different stopping-out varnish may be used for retouching that does not contain any beeswax such as molten asphalt powder with turpentine or black spirit varnish.

The hot-plate

To apply the ground to the plate the latter must be warmed. It should not be too cold or the ground will not melt; if it is too hot, it will be burnt. To determine this well we need a hot-plate whose temperature can be regulated; this means preferably a plate heated by electricity or gas. A very good method is to use a broad iron plate, which can be heated in one place while another part remains more or less cold. When the ground is well distributed we move the etching plate quickly to the cold part; the ground then solidifies quite quickly, which is important for keeping it free from dust.

The dabber

To spread the ground really evenly over the plate we need a dabber, or a leather or rubber roller. We also need a dabber for inking the plate. For the ground, it is covered with fine-mesh silk and for inking with soft leather. Cut a disc of stiff cardboard with a diameter of about 7 to 8 cm (about 3 in), make a firm ball of horsehair or greasy cotton wool, put it on the cardboard, stretch the silk all round, and draw it tight. The piece of silk must be large enough to leave sufficient for a handle. This is made by winding string round it. A roller is also satisfactory; the rubber roller must be soft and resilient. Both dabbers and rollers may be bought.

Applying the etching ground

The plate must now be given a thin layer of etching ground. It is important for this to be done properly, since a poorly applied ground will not respond as it should. If it is too thin places will be etched where this was not the intention. If it is too thick the layer is likely to crumble at intersections of lines. This also happens if the ground is burnt by excessive heat; it then becomes brittle and peels off the plate when this is drawn on with the etching needle. The same thing takes place when the plate is in the acid bath. If we draw a line with the needle through a thin and a thicker part of the ground, the acid encounters more resistance in the thick part, so that the line becomes thinner and shallower. We then clearly see the division between the thin and thicker layer of ground in a large batch of lines. We also see this very well on the print. The ground must therefore be applied as uniformly as possible. Dust is probably its worst enemy; the wax layer draws away round the dust particles when the plate is warm. We can see this clearly under the magnifying glass. Not more than one-quarter of the ground that normally lies on the plate gathers round the dust particle. The acid bites through quickly here, so that dozens of little holes are bitten in the plate. We do not see this immediately, and sometimes it does not matter very much if black pits are visible on the print. But it may well be undesirable, and then it is a real problem to get rid of the holes.

The plate does not need to be warmed for the application of the liquid ground. Set the plate down at an oblique angle. Pour some liquid ground from the bottle into a saucer. It must not be thick as treacle, but must flow easily; nor must it be too thin, or the acid will soon bite through it. If it is too thick it may be diluted with turpentine or turpentine substitute, or in some cases with petrol. Take a soft, dust-free brush and put on the ground in bands from top to bottom just as though you were applying a good, even ground of water-colour. Dust is even more troublesome than with a solid ground. Here too, the ground will adhere round the dust particle.

The above method must be learnt by frequent practice. The following is an easier way. Hold the plate from below and in the centre on the fingertips and pour a dash of liquid ground onto the middle. With an upward and downward turning motion cause the liquid to run slowly to the four corners; this soon produces an even surface. The ground is not hard until the turpentine substitute has evaporated. This sometimes takes a couple of hours; the plate should therefore be laid carefully in a horizontal position in a cupboard, so that no dust can fall on it. We may also lay it on a lukewarm hot-plate or use a hair-drier.

Smoking the etching plate

When the plate is covered by a thin layer of ground the artist draws in it with the etching needle. But the layer is so thin that the gloss of the polished plate usually impedes the work. Moreover, the lines are difficult to see if the needle is very fine. Those who etch a great deal are used to this and do not need a layer of soot. Nearly all plates were smoked at one time before the artist drew on them, and it is still done. We need a good smoky flame. A thick twisted tallow candle or a well turned-up smoky wick of an oil cooker are excellent for coating the plate with soot. A firm ball of cotton wool soaked in oil and tied on a knitting needle may also be used. Holding the plate a couple of centimetres (roughly an inch) away from the flame melts the ground, which accepts directly and mixes with the particles of soot. To hold the plate firm, it should be clamped in a hand vice between two pieces of cardboard so as not to damage the layer of wax. When the plate has cooled it can be stroked with the hand without rubbing off the coating.

Drawing on the etching plate

If we wish to copy a drawing as accurately as possible we must transfer the outlines to the etching plate. The back of the draw-ing may be rubbed with white or coloured chalk, which is, as it were, printed on. In this case we subsequently obtain the mirror image on the print. If this is not desired, then the object must be printed on the plate in mirror image. Draw the outlines with a soft chalk on the glass of an illuminator or against the light of a window, lay the drawn side on the etching plate and rub over it vigorously with the hand.

Many artists prefer to use the drawing for guidance only, con-sulting it now and again. Others draw directly on the plate. No instructions can be given for the latter; everyone will do it differently. The needle must pass everywhere through the ground. We must find a middle way between a soft caress and a harsh scratch. But we must pay attention to other things as well. When the plate is in the acid bath the etching process will more or less alter the line. The acid, at any rate nitric acid, not only bites downwards, but also sideways. It undermines the side edges of the drawn line, and it does this more severely the longer the plate lies in the acid. The strength and the temperature also play a part. If the lines are bitten for a fairly short time we may ignore their undermining. But broader lines that are bitten deep will become still broader.

If the lines are drawn too close together so that the ridges between them are very narrow, then the latter will obviously be undermined and soon disappear altogether. This is the reason for the "dead areas" on the etching. Anyone who etches a great deal sees dead areas immediately; they hold very little if any ink when the plate is wiped. If, for example, three or four lines are bitten into a broad band by under-etching and we wipe the plate clean, for example with gauze and then once more with the base of the hand, then we rub over the bottom of a line that is much too broad and remove too much ink. If there are one or two islands (ridges) in this over-broad line, then our hand will not rub the bottom and the ink will remain in it.

There are many possible ways of drawing on the ground. We may finish the drawing on the ground in one go with thin and thick needles. By etching for a longer or a shorter time (from half a minute to an hour or even longer), a large number of variations can be made in breadth and depth. We must remove the plate from the bath, rinse it, dry it and cover the parts that are not to be bitten any more with stopping-out varnish, liquid ground or black spirit varnish.

The parts to be stopped-out must be covered very well, for the ground has the disconcerting habit of dripping off the edges of the etched line. We can see under the magnifying glass that these edges have retained no more than one quarter of the thickness in other places. In the beginning this is not thought of, or the danger is underestimated.

When the plate is lying in the bath for already bitten lines to be subjected to further action we see whole rows of small gas bubbles on these edges. If these edges are etched unevenly, this will obviously be at the expense of the already etched line. It is

The etcher's tools (needle, scraper and dabber)

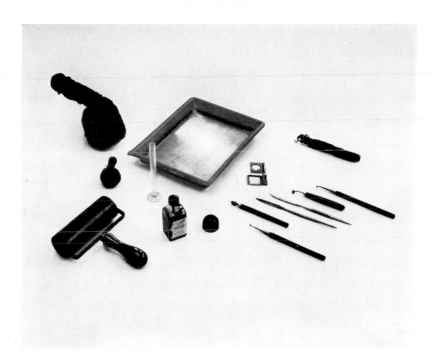

The author makes a drawing in sugar aquatint

Detail of *The Three Crosses* by Rembrandt (second state, 38·6 × 45·2 cm; 15·2 × 17·8 in)

The same detail. The plate has been scraped and worked with the dry-point needle (fourth state)

The Three Crosses by Rembrandt (fourth state, 38·6 × 45·2 cm; 15·2 × 17·8 in)

Dry-point; the plate is scratched with the needle, when the burr remains

Dry-point

best to coat these parts twice with stopping-out varnish, black spirit varnish or shellac. Another method is as follows. First etch the heavy, deep lines, and then, during the etching process, draw in additional lines, which will then not be bitten for so long. We avoid in this way the dangers of the former method. Some prefer this method, while others like the other one best.

The acid bath and etching on zinc and copper

As a general rule, any acids that attack and corrode zinc and copper may be used. Most etchers use nitric acid. Its strength depends on various factors. When cold, nitric acid etches slowly, and a solution of 30 per cent may be too weak. In hot summer weather, when the etching bath is lukewarm, 10 per cent is too strong. A second important factor is the variation of the temperature during etching. If we etch a large number of lines at the same time and many gas bubbles are formed, the temperature rises rapidly.

At normal room temperature we may start with a 15 per cent nitric acid solution. The strength of the nitric acid must be known when it is purchased; it will usually be 50 per cent or 80 per cent. Gas bubbles form during the etching process when nitric acid is used for the bath. Not very much happens below these bubbles, and so we must remove them with a feather or a dish mop made of thick cotton threads. If we do not do this, the plate will still be etched, since the bubbles will burst in time. But etching will take at least twice as long.

Some etchers use iron perchloride, which is also a good etching liquor. It has the disadvantage that it is not so easy to see how the plate is being etched; this must be discovered by experiment. Iron perchloride may be purchased in solution, but it is cheaper if bought in lumps; these may be left to stand in water for a day. The writer has etched zinc plates in 8 to 12 minutes in a saturated solution; a normal line is then bitten. But it is advisable for etching on zinc and copper to make trial plates first and remember well what happened with them. The prints from them are good material for the budding etcher; this applies not only to line-etching, but also to all the etching techniques still to follow.

There is a great difference between nitric acid and iron perchloride; the latter bites mainly in depth. The broadening of the lines that takes place with nitric acid is not nearly so marked a feature of iron perchloride. In practice this difference means that very thin lines bitten in nitric acid are very shallow and therefore hold less ink. The same lines etched with iron perchloride are just as narrow, but they are deeper and hold more ink; they produce a more pithy line on the print, and this may be necessary. How it comes about that iron perchloride has this property does not matter very much to the artist, as long as he knows how to make use of it. It seems that the etching liquor leaves a kind of deposit on the side edges of the bitten line, so that the metal there is no longer attacked.

For an etching on a copper plate, we may use a strong solution of nitric acid, but a special composition is still better. The following is a good recipe:

3 parts by weight of potassium chloride,
20 parts by weight of hydrochloric acid,
75 parts by weight of water.

The hydrochloric acid is the most important ingredient. First dissolve the potassium chloride in the warm water, and then add the hydrochloric acid.

A single etching is not usually enough to complete the job. A proof or experience will show that some parts are not etched deeply enough, while others are. If the plate is not yet clean, then the matter is very simple; after stopping-out here and there the plate goes back into the acid bath.

If we discover this after stripping the ground off the plate, we cannot, of course, put the latter back in the acid bath. In such cases we take a hard rubber roller. We cannot treat the plate with a ball of ground, since this would fill the lines. We therefore warm a clean piece of zinc, apply the ball of ground to it, and roll the rubber roller in it. This ground-coated roller is then passed carefully over the warmed, already etched plate. The ground is not intended to enter the lines; the roller only touches the surface of the plate between them. If we use a soft roller and press too hard the ground will flow into the lines. When the plate has cooled, we brush stopping-out varnish on all the parts that have been well bitten. Before the plate is placed in the bath we look at the back again to ensure that no large areas of unprotected zinc are visible. If everything has gone according to plan, we clean the plate with turpentine substitute and spirit, and we can then start printing.

Aquatint

So far we have only discussed pure line-etching in which grey parts are obtained by fine, thin etched lines, which may intersect. The aquatint technique enables us to produce these grey tones in an entirely different way. The principle of etching is that lines and dots are etched in the plate, these are filled with ink, the plate is wiped clean again, and the ink remains in the lines and dots. According to the aquatint technique, dozens of little dots and rings are etched in the plate.

We need various ingredients for this; resin and asphalt powder are excellent. Suppose we wish to have tones varying from light to very dark grey in a given part of the etching. The plate, already etched with lines if desired, is placed on the work table. A box of resin powder stands close by. We take a piece of muslin or an old nylon stocking, put resin powder in it, and make a ball as big as a medium-sized apple; then we tie this up with string.

We make two of these balls. We knock them together over the etching plate, on to which a fine rain of resin powder falls. The way we knock the balls together decides how much powder will fall onto the plate. We must not let too much powder land on it, since the particles will fuse together if they are too close to each other. The intention is to hold the plate above a gas flame or place it on a hot-plate so that the particles of resin melt. If the particles of resin fuse together we get a resin cake, and then nothing happens when we start etching. When the resin particles are fixed (this does not take very long), we stop-out any parts that are not to be etched with black spirit varnish or some other stopping-out varnish. We then put the plate in a bath containing a solution of nitric acid of about 15 per cent strength. The acid etches *round* the resin particles, because the resin is acid-resistant. Nothing happens below them; the copper or zinc is not attacked.

Various points demand attention here. Not all the particles of resin are of the same size. We know that the acid undermines the ground, but this also applies to the resin particles. The very smallest will therefore soon disappear. We may stop-out parts as with line-etching and etch the remainder again. If we clean the plate with spirit and turpentine substitute, then we see that the metal has been etched away round the resin particles, so that a large number of small and not so small rings have formed. By coarser scattering, for example by rubbing the powder between the fingers or using a screen of coarser tissue, we can cause resin particles of very different sizes to fall onto the plate and produce very wonderful aquatint parts.

Sometimes a really even aquatint has to be etched. It is very difficult to do this in the way we have just described. This method produces an uneven, picturesque effect, which is why many artists prefer hand-dusting. To make an even aquatint, we must go to work more mechanically. The etching plate must be placed in a space filled with innumerable resin particles, which whirl round and slowly settle. We can easily make one of these aquatint boxes ourselves, especially if we use small etching plates. We knock up two frames measuring, for example, 40 x 40 cm (15 in x 15 in). Then we make a high cardboard box without a bottom or top, which fits in the two frames, one at the bottom and one at the top to keep the whole together. We attach the frames a few centimetres below the edges, and the aquatint box is ready.

We put the etching plate at the end of a table, at the other end of which stands the aquatint box. Then we take two firm balls of resin powder and knock them together over the box. We pick up the latter, put it carefully over the plate, and lay a sheet of paper on the top opening. After a minute or rather less, we lift the box and find that a thin layer of resin powder has settled very unevenly on the plate. The heaviest particles of resin will settle first, and so plenty of very fine particles will still be floating in the air after the first minute. If we have another plate on which a fine tone is to be produced, we put the box over it. It will take a good quarter of an hour before all the particles have settled. We now have two plates with resin powder after only one dusting.

Of course, this is a primitive system, and powder settles beside the box as well as in it, so that the whole of the studio or room will be dusty. It is therefore better to make an aquatint box that does not leak. For this, take a cardboard or wooden box, that is a cube stuck tight at all the edges. Make a slot of 3 cm ($1\frac{1}{4}$ in) in the side, 2 cm ($\frac{3}{4}$ in) above the bottom, over the entire breadth or rather less. Put four laths on the bottom, each 2 cm ($\frac{3}{4}$ in) broad. Then make a frame out of laths for standing the etching plate on. It must be small enough for it to be pushed easily into the box through the slot together with the plate. The slot must then be closed with a hinged lath. Now make a round hole of $1\frac{1}{2}$ cm ($\frac{1}{2}$ in) on one of the sides, and insert a blowpipe through it.

Scatter a couple of ounces of resin powder through the slot, and the aquatint box is ready for use. Put the plate on the frame, close the slot, and blow on to the bottom through the blowpipe; this can also be done with bellows or, if the box is not too large, by turning it over and setting it down again. Open the flap quickly, and put in the frame with the plate on it. Then wait a minute or so; the exact time depends on the amount of resin powder in the box. Next, carefully remove the frame with the plate.

Here too, experience must teach us whether there is too much or too little resin on the plate. Examination under a magnifying glass clearly shows the zinc or copper with the grains of resin on it. For a normal aquatint we must see about 70 per cent of resin. If we see a great deal of metal and a grain of resin here and there, then we should repeat the process. It should be remembered that the finest particles of resin will soon disappear in the acid bath.

Anything can be improved, including an aquatint box. Start with a box as described above and on both sides, exactly in the middle, put an iron peg at least 1 cm ($\frac{2}{5}$in) thick. It would naturally be easier to push a round iron rod crosswise through the box. But this cannot be done. The rod must not be allowed in the box, because the resin would settle on the rod when it is turned round, and would fall off here and there in small flakes onto our plate. For we are making a rotary aquatint box. The two projecting pegs are hung in a stand, and the closed box can now be turned without letting resin out of it. Do not turn too quickly; if you do, centrifugal force will prevent the desired effect, and the aim is for the air box to be full of whirling particles of resin. When the box is in the correct position we must fix it with a clip or hook.

Large etchings require a large box; it may be made collapsible, so that it can be kept in the studio like a portfolio. A dust-sucker may be used instead of a blowpipe. Asphalt powder may be used instead of a blowpipe. Asphalt powder may be used instead of resin; it is finer, but has the advantage over resin that it is readily visible.

When the plate has been taken out of the aquatint box it must be heated as soon as possible. Beware of draughts in the room you are working in. The hundreds of thousands of particles of resin lie loose on the plate; one jolt or breath of air, and everything is ruined. The plate may be put on the hot-plate, when the fine grains will soon be fixed, or held over a gas flame. The aquatint will be damaged by holding it with tongs. With a little skill the plate can be held between the hands, first one half and then the other. The best method, especially for large plates for which the hot-plate is too small, is a metal frame attached to the wall; the grained plate is put on this very carefully. The flame may be held under the plate with the aid of a gas poker or copper pipe on the end of a rubber tube, when the resin grains will be seen to melt.

The above also applies to aquatints made with asphalt. Asphalt grains are much finer and more acid-resistant, and they produce much finer aquatints. But asphalt does not melt so quickly as resin. If asphalt is heated rather too much it will be burned on to the plate so firmly that it will not dissolve readily later on.

The following procedure may be followed by those who have no aquatint box, but wish to make a uniform aquatint. Put a few spoonfuls of asphalt powder in a bottle half-full of alcohol. Asphalt does not dissolve in alcohol. If the bottle is shaken all the asphalt particles will sink to the bottom. Do this, and squirt on to the etching plate with a fixing nozzle. A fine layer of asphalt particles will stick to the plate quite evenly. The alcohol vaporizes immediately. Heat the plate, and the asphalt will be fixed. The writer prefers this method to pouring the liquid over the plate.

Resin and asphalt may be used in combination. If a very dark aquatint is wanted, an asphalt aquatint is applied first. When this has been bitten correctly, clean the plate, but scatter a layer of resin over it by hand or in the aquatint box. The resin particles are larger than the asphalt ones. Fix the resin particles, and put the plate back in the acid bath. Nothing happens to the resin particles; an ordinary resin aquatint results, except that a much finer asphalt aquatint lies beneath the resin grains. The combination of the two results in a maximum of fine holes, which ensure a velvety black print.

To make a very fine aquatint, the plate should not be placed in the box immediately, but you should wait for half a minute to allow the largest asphalt grains to fall to the bottom and the very fine ones to go on to the plate. It is advisable to repeat this several times before warming the latter. If you are going to etch, try all this out on trial plates. The possibilities are almost inexhaustible.

Salt aquatint

The salt aquatint is another variant. The procedure is exactly the opposite to that used for the resin or asphalt aquatint. A rather softer etching ground is rolled on to the plate. The ball of ground is pressed on to the hot plate, and a small amount (one-quarter) of beeswax or hard fat is added. The whole is mixed well with the rubber roller. The ground is now rather more soft. When the plate has cooled, fine cooking salt is scattered on it. The plate is warmed again, the ground melts, and the salt particles sink. When the plate has cooled, all the parts that are not to be etched must be stopped-out. The salt particles melt in the etching liquor, enabling the acid to bite the zinc away in the opened holes. Small pits are formed. This aquatint has quite a different character from that of the resin aquatint, which is composed entirely of unequal rings.

Sugar aquatint

Aquatint may be used in many ways; those who wish to employ

a picturesque etching technique can produce with it etchings having the effect of a drawing in crayon. Think what you like about this; we are only mentioning the technical possibilities.

We dissolve some ordinary sugar in water; it must not become a thick treacle, but we must be able to apply it easily with a brush. We mix some black poster paint with this colourless sugar solution. If we now draw with a brush on a plate free from grease we get a smooth brush stroke. But if the plate is rather greasy (this may be caused by merely stroking it with the hand), then the sugar solution will contract, and we get a rough, frayed line, which fails to "take" on the zinc in some places. This is exactly what is wanted in the present case. When the drawing is finished, it should first be dried well. This may take one or two hours, although the process can, of course, be speeded up by putting it on the hot-plate or using hot air. When the plate is well dried, we put it down at an inclined angle, and apply a thin layer of liquid ground over it evenly from top to bottom, so that the dried sugar solution is also covered. When the ground is dry, we put the plate in a bath of lukewarm water and rub the plate with a wad of cotton wool. The sugar with the ground on it is soon released. The sugar solution lines are visible as light zinc on the somewhat dark plate. If this plate were put in the etching bath now, the lines would become much too broad, so that we should remove too much ink from them on wiping the plate and get dull, grey lines. An aquatint is therefore laid over the lines. This may be done with a dusting tube, aquatint box, or a bag. Scatter more roughly, and you will enhance the character of the sugar-aquatint technique. The plate should then be warmed again to melt the resin. This process may be combined with etching lines.

The greasy-crayon technique

An entirely different process is the greasy-crayon technique and drawing with etching ground on the plate. The method may be summarized by the description, "working with acid-resistant material". The following may be used: etching ground, stopping-out varnish, spirit varnish, lithographic crayon and wax crayon. Other materials may well be suitable too. Wherever this material has been applied to the etching plate and in whatever manner, the latter is not attacked. The acid cannot penetrate it. Of course, lines may be etched or aquatints applied subsequently in different places.

Lithographic crayon in particular gives very good results, but some time should be spent on experimenting to learn the possibilities of this technique. Lithographic pencils are most suitable for this. We must remember that all the lines will be printed white. As we already know, the nitric acid bath undermines the ground to some extent if we draw with the etching needle. This also happens if we draw lines on the etching plate with a lithographic pencil; they become thicker or thinner with longer or shorter etching. The side of a piece of lithographic crayon may also be used for drawing on the plate and even for etching tones similar to aquatint.

It is best to use unpolished plates. A plate treated in this way must, of course, be etched with nitric acid for only a very short time. When it has been etched for 30 seconds or a minute, it may be rinsed, dried, and treated with greasy crayon again. To make the latter more resistant to the acid, some asphalt powder may be spread over it with a wad of cotton wool; the crayon takes up the very fine asphalt powder.

The soft-ground technique

This technique is a fairly old one; it was probably employed by Hercules Seghers. A soft ground is used, with which some wax, mutton fat or tallow is mixed. This may be bought in small porcelain pots, mixed with lavender oil. Its quality is excellent, so that there is no need to make it yourself. Take some from a pot with a knife point, and spread it on the warmed plate with a soft rubber roller. If you have not got a pot of soft ground, you can do the same thing quite easily in a different way. When the plate is polished, warm it, press the ball of ground several times on to it, and put a piece of fat on it. Roll with the rubber roller for a long time to mix the ground thoroughly. When we have a good, thin layer of ground on the plate and the latter is cool, it may be treated in a number of different ways.

The following procedure generally used to be employed, and still is. A piece of paper, preferably with a coarse structure, such as water-colour or very coarse wrapping paper, is laid on the cooled soft ground. If we draw on the paper with a pencil, the texture of the paper is printed through the soft layer of varnish. The paper must be secured to prevent it from slipping. When the drawing is ready, the paper is removed, the back of the plate is stopped-out, and the plate is put in the etching bath, which must not be too strong; the gas bubbles forming on the lines may be carefully removed with a feather. To give a large area a layer of a given texture, various materials may be used, such as linen, curtaining or nylon stockings. The first finest textures can be etched in the plate by the proper use of this technique.

Tools for etchers and engravers

The tools we need for etching will easily fit in the inside pocket of a suit. First of all, we require some etching needles, a scraper, a burnisher, perhaps a whetstone, a rubber or composition roller, and a dabber for laying the ground. For printing, we need a sharp-cut piece of rubber sheeting, a dabber, muslin, and finally a couple of felt blankets. The etching needles have already been dealt with.

A burnisher and scraper are indispensable. In spite of all precautions, undesired holes and other damage are bound to appear on the plate here and there. It may also be found that an entire part must be removed later on. If so, take your scraper, which is a triangular scraping knife ending in a sharp point, and which must always be kept razor-sharp; it is a dangerous instrument, and so it is kept with a cork on the point. The area to be taken out is scraped with one of the three edges. We merely remove a layer of zinc or copper. It is assumed in this case that the lines or aquatint to be scraped away are etched deep. When they have almost disappeared, the burnisher or, if the area is large, the whetstone, is used. The whole area is polished smooth with some oil or grease. The removal of such a large area is a major operation, and some experience is needed to do it properly. As a rule, however, only small corrections are required.

An interesting example is a plate by Hercules Seghers, *Tobias and the Angel*, two large figures in a mountainous landscape. Rembrandt obtained this plate; with or without Seghers' consent, he scraped the figures away and etched *The Flight into Egypt* on top. Careful examination of Rembrandt's etching shows distinctly the remains of a tree. The famous *Three Crosses* by Rembrandt has also been practically entirely scraped away, polished and gone over again with the dry-point needle.

Printing the plate

The first thing we do when we are going to take the first proof is damp the paper. We do not often etch a plate entirely without taking a proof. Every artist naturally has his own way of printing; some take many proofs, while others do not take any. In any case, we must not underestimate the preparation of the paper. We are curious to see what the first proof will look like, and are inclined to be not very particular over the printing. But the writer advises very great care with the proof, for it must show us the exact state of affairs, and it must guide us in making any improvements. The aquatint may be too dark here and too light there, or the lines may not turn out as expected.

Printing etchings in the twentieth and seventeenth centuries

Home-made aquatint box in use

Filing and scouring

Grounding with a ball of ground and dabber

Smoking the plate

Drawing in the ground

Etching

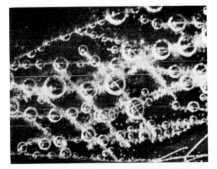

Formation of gas when etching
(enlarged detail)

Application of ink with the dabber

Dusting with resin powder for the aquatint technique

Pressing jute into the soft ground (soft-ground technique)

Several things are essential in any case for printing. First and foremost, we need a press. With woodcuts, a spoon and a key or a paperknife are adequate. Etching and lithography are a different story, and a press is essential. It is true that a detail can be printed very laboriously without one, by covering the damp paper with a layer of felt and then rubbing a hard object over it; but etchings cannot be printed in this way.

An etching press consists of two steel cylinders, the bottom one usually having a larger diameter than the top one. The top cylinder of the writer's press has a diameter of 25 cm (10 in) and weighs 300 kg (666 lb). But it is one of the heaviest types. A press with cylinders 60 cm (24 in) long and diameters of 12 to 15 cm (5 to 6 in) is very suitable. The force needed to pass the etching plate between the rollers can be reduced considerably, sometimes 25 times, by using a system of wheels. However, small steel presses are excellent. The cylinders are made of steel, but they used to be made of very hard wood. Some of these presses may be seen in the Plantijnmuseum, Antwerp. There is also a press with wooden cylinders in the Rembrandthuis, Amsterdam. The old Dutch presses usually had oak cylinders, with a four-armed cross for turning the rollers. The press in the Rembrandthuis is beech and has a six-armed cross. The two cylinders have different centre lines. The bottom roller, which must take the pressure, has a *lignum vitae* surface. The top one has a *lignum vitae* core and a walnut surface. The pressure of the cylinders must be readily adjustable, and there must be some resilience between them; this can be achieved by putting a spring or pile of cardboard on either side of the press. This resilience is necessary to take up any excessive pressure, uniformity of which must be regulated by it. The gap between the cylinders must be the same everywhere.

An etching press is not an article in great demand produced on a conveyor belt. New presses are expensive, and it is advisable to consult an expert before procuring one; the same applies to second-hand presses. A cobbler's press may be used with a few small modifications. An old-fashioned mangle is not so suitable; its pressure cannot be raised enough to give us good, sound prints; it may be used for a small etching, but not so easily for a larger one. There is quite a different kind of press on which etchings can be printed with quite good results; this is the lithographic press. If we procure one, usually second-hand, we kill two birds with one stone; we can print both etchings and lithographs, though we cannot print the latter with an etching press.

Printing an etching on a lithographic press

We shall return to the lithographic press when discussing that technique. When we have prepared the etching plate for printing, we first lay a fairly thick stone on the press, and then a sheet of unprinted paper. We lay the plate in the middle of the stone. We lay the damp paper on the plate in the usual way, and then two layers of resilient felt. Now comes the difference to the etching press; we lay on the felt a plate of zinc about $1\frac{1}{2}$ mm thick. The plate must be very smooth; this can be aided by oiling it, making the surface as slippery as possible. We move the sliding bed up to a couple of centimetres before the etching plate below the scraper. We set the pressure at the top or bottom according to the design. And then we pass the plate through. If the paper, the felt and the pressure are good, we get an irreproachable print. The writer is not relying on hearsay; he has done it himself for years, even with etchings measuring 50 x 65 cm (20 x 26 in). With "block zinc", or zinc 2 mm thick, the plate may not pass underneath when it has reached the scraper. A facet must be ground on a thick etching plate so that the plate may gradually pass through. If a facet is not desired, then a strip of zinc as thick as the etching plate may be laid before the latter; the zinc strip then acts as a bridge. During printing on the lithographic press, the zinc "tympan" has a tendency to become rounded; with each printing operation we must bend it straight again, although in time this will be found to be no longer necessary.

The paper

Besides art paper, any type may be used. This does not mean that all are equally good. The writer once printed three hundred etchings on wrapping paper two hundred years old containing small stones, sand and all manner of other iniquities. He first removed the coarsest obstacles, but everything then went excellently. Paper containing wood must not be used in any circumstances, and the paper must not be sized too much; blotting or filter paper absorbs too much moisture; soft drawing or watercolour paper is suitable.

Some factories have brought out a special etching paper. Van Gelder's copper-intaglio paper is good, but it absorbs a great deal of water. It is advisable to damp it a few hours before using it and to leave it under pressure between a couple of dry sheets of paper; it is soft, and if a large sheet has to be damped it is liable to tear. In such cases it is best to lay the sheet on a drawing-board or some other wooden board and hold the whole under the tap; this will not tear the paper. The thick *simili japon* paper is also good, but it tends to turn yellow in time. The etching paper by Hahne Mülle in sheets measuring 50 x 65 cm (20 x 26 in) is very good. It is also obtainable in double dimensions and double thickness. It is important to damp the paper well. A good method is to damp it on both sides and repeat this process after a quarter of an hour, when it will have lost its stretch. The paper is then laid between two sheets of glass or kept for some time between two wet cloths or wet sheets of paper. Before printing, we should hold it against the light for a moment to see whether it has any dry patches.

The felt

The felt for the blankets must be of good quality; this applies, of course, to all the materials, but particularly to the felt. It must not be too thick; 3 to 4 mm is adequate. If it is too thin it is not resilient enough to press the paper into the lines. Two or three superimposed layers are better than one thick one; we then have the advantage that the blankets can be changed.

If a large number of prints are taken the felt is crushed; with each print it becomes rather damp, and the moisture contains gum from the paper. In time the felt will become hard and lose its resilience. When this happens, the print is liable to have white lines here and there where black ones were intended. Care must also be taken that no dirt or ink gets onto the felt. If the felt has become hard and thin and has lost its resilience, then it should be beaten, brushed, "kneaded" and massaged. After half an hour it has become so beautifully supple again that we no longer recognize it. It may also be soaked in water for one night and then washed with soft soap, rinsed well, dried and rubbed loosely between the hands. The writer has also successfully washed a very old blanket in a washing machine. The felt may be obtained from a wholesaler for the graphic industry.

Inking the plate

When we are ready to print the etching plate, our first task is to get the ink right. We need a special ink for etching; it must be easy to apply to the plate and also easy to wipe off again. Viscous, treacly ink is unsuitable. We may, of course, make it ourselves, but there are some first-class copper-intaglio inks on the market. If the ink is rather too stiff, it may be diluted with boiled linseed oil, or better still with stand oil. Some etchers add a little oil paint, some Prussian blue or carmine, which gives a more intense black impression. Others mix in some emerald green. Use one or two drops of drying agent only if the lines are too deeply etched. We do not need one for a normal etching.

There is no harm in wiping the lines with a rag soaked in linseed oil before inking begins. The plate then becomes rather greasy, and releases the ink better when it comes off the press; this need not be repeated for every print. For inking, we have a special dabber, which is used only for this operation. Rubbing in with the fingertip is best for small etching plates. Another method is to rub the printing ink into the lines with a piece of rubber and remove the surplus printing ink. If we have no rubber, then a sharp piece of passe-partout paper is also suitable. We then wipe the plate clean with muslin, tarlatan, curtaining, bandaging or paper-hanger's linen. All the ink will not be removed in this way; we must ensure that some remains in the lines and the aquatint. The plate is still not clean enough after this treatment; it is now "finish-wiped" by hand. We wipe some of the ink off the plate with the flat hand. This is repeated until there is no longer any surplus ink on the plate.

At the end of this treatment we rub some chalk powder into our hands, which we clap together so that no loose grains remain on them. It is important for the hand to be quite dry. We wipe the plate again, and the very thin chalk layer removes all surplus ink. It goes without saying that we can only learn to wipe by doing it several times; this applies to all etching operations. The whole wiping operation is carried out best on a warmed plate; the ink then becomes softer and is easier to wipe off.

Another successful method is based on the following principle: in intaglio printing, the ink lies in the depth of the etched or engraved line. If the line is filled to the brim with ink, so that no more can be added, and if paper and felt are laid on it, the paper will press into line, and the ink will then be forced out of the line, since the paper cannot absorb it rapidly enough. Ugly, outflowing lines will be formed. But they are not entirely filled on wiping by our treatment of the plate; actually, the bottoms are well filled. As a result, the damp paper is pressed to the bottom of the line and yet ink does not flow out. If we look at the wrong side of the etching, we see clearly that the paper is pressed into the lines. Those on the right side lie on the paper-like wires. The deeper they are etched, the thicker they will be. These lines are actually 80 per cent paper. That does not matter, there is nothing against it, and an etching like this can be a great work of art. But some etchers regard this paper line as a kind of fraud. In their view, the line must consist of ink.

The etcher A. Schotel has developed his own method for obeying this principle of the ink line. This is demonstrated in detail in a film, *The Black Dabber*. The plate is oiled, so as to cover the lines with a thin layer. A special ink made by the etcher himself is inserted in the lines with a well-polished putty knife. The plate is then not wiped clean with muslin in the usual way. Instead, the etcher shaves it with a razor blade mounted on a wooden block. This makes it fairly clean, but not clean enough to produce a clear print. It would not be appropriate with this method to wipe clean with the hand to remove the last residues of surplus ink. A special tool which does this for the artist has been designed for wiping. A strip of paper from a roller slides slowly over the etching; this strip is more than 100 metres long for one etching. Meanwhile, a leather pad presses the paper gently now and then. After a couple of minutes the plate is removed from the tool and is then found to be completely free from all surplus ink. The ink now "floats" on the thin layer of oil.

The press is also adapted to this system; the top cylinder is not made of steel in the usual way, but of rubber. The pressure is much less than with metal cylinders. This is necessary because the line is completely filled with ink and only needs to adhere to the paper, which does not press into the line. As the line is first oiled, the adhesion to the paper is strong enough to lift the line out of the groove.

According to the inventor of this technique, success may be

achieved not only with the special ink he makes himself and the oil that he distils himself. Something similar, although perhaps not quite so perfect, may be accomplished much more simply with an ordinary inked plate.

After wiping with muslin, we take a number of strips of paper; printed or unprinted newspaper is best. We draw a strip with one hand over the lukewarm rotary plate, and with the other hand we execute a rotary, pressing motion. After we have drawn four or five strips over the plate in this way, the latter is completely free from ink. Fine aquatints can also be printed in this way with a little experience.

Corrections after printing

We now return to the usual printing method. We lay a sheet of clean paper, which is rather larger than the etching paper, on the steel plate possessed by every etching press. On this we put the inked plate. We now place the damp paper on the latter and then at least two blankets, and we pass the plate through the press. The etching is now rather firmly stuck. To remove the print easily, the plate is warmed. An examination of the print may show that some alterations are necessary. When we have cleaned the plate with turpentine substitute, we may make all kinds of small corrections.

We make an aquatint box to insert aquatints locally. We half-fill a jam pot or tin with resin powder or asphalt powder and tie a fine-mesh cloth over the bottom. Already applied aquatints may be made darker in this way. If an aquatint is too dark, then we can make its topmost points smooth with fine abrasive paper, polishing paper or a burnisher, producing a lighter tone on printing. Some parts can also be made darker with the dry-point needle, or the plate may be ground again and fresh parts etched.

If we take several proofs after the various treatments, then we call them the first, second, third or fourth state, etc. If an etching has been printed and is still damp, it is best to lay it between two sheets of strawboard and put a heavy weight on top. If the print has thick lines, it is better to hang it up to dry. When the ink is dry, damp the etching and mount it with strong adhesive tape.

SURFACE PRINTING
(LITHOGRAPHY)

Origins

THE technique of lithography is not so old as wood-cutting, etching or engraving. It is based on quite a different principle: chemical action. Invented in 1798 by Alois Senefelder, it is the only printing method whose inventor is known with certainty. It is not an improvement of any process, but something quite new. Senefelder was not looking for a new graphic method, but wished to reproduce his music and writings so that he would be independent of printers. In his *Manual of Lithography*, which contains everything on the subject, he wrote, "You will then be able to print the products of your mind for yourselves, give yourselves a proper existence and become free and independent men." This desire to print his poems, plays and music himself was only the immediate cause of the invention of lithography.

Senefelder started by experimenting with the printing methods known to him again and again, until he remarked one day, "I was brought still closer to the new invention by the following experiment. When I had damped by dipping in water, on which a few drops of linseed oil were floating, a sheet with dried greasy lithographic drawing ink on it, I found that this oil adhered uniformly to the writing, while the rest of the paper did not accept any oil, especially if it was damped with gum water or thin starch. This induced me to try to see how paper would behave when printed with ordinary printing ink. A printed page from an old book was passed through diluted gum water, then laid on a stone, and sponged well all over with a piece of sponge dipped in thin oil paint. The printed letters accepted the ink well everywhere, and the paper itself remained white. I then laid another sheet of white paper on top, passed both through the press and obtained a good copy of the printed page in mirror image. In this way I was able with care to take fifty or more copies from the same sheet."

After this success he continued with his tests. "I took a well-ground stone, drew on it with a piece of soap, poured thin gum water over it, and passed over it a sponge dipped in oil paint. All the places that had been marked with greasy soap became black directly, while the rest remained white. I could print from the stone as often as I wished."

Subsequently, Senefelder greatly improved his new method by etching and preparing the stone with nitric acid, so that he could take an unlimited number of prints. Nobody thought in those first years of lithography that it would turn out to be an important technique for graphic artists. It was some time before a real art of lithographic prints arose. Although the technique was invented in Germany, and Germany has produced some great lithographers, such as Max Liebermann, Menzel and Käthe Kollwitz, France is without doubt the home of the lithographer. In the first period Géricault and Delacroix turned out numerous specimens of this art. Goya also made four great lithographs at Bordeaux. But the golden age begins with the prolific Honoré Daumier. Satire was his forte. He worked for a number of journals, such as *Le Charivari*, for which he made many lithographic drawings. But it was not only Daumier who made France the home of the lithographer; a part was also played by Fantin Latour, Odilon Redon, Toulouse-Lautrec and dozens of others.

In the Netherlands, there is quite an old lithographic print (1809) made by S. Petit. But at the end of the nineteenth century a number of capable lithographers appeared in the Netherlands, such as Weissenburch, Jan Veth and Van Hoytema.

The technique of lithography

In surface printing the ink is on the same level as the part that is not to be printed. The process is based on the acceptance and rejection of the ink, or to put it another way, grease and non-grease. To make the lithograph as successful as possible, the opposition between acceptance and rejection is made as strong as can be.

Lithographic stones are porous, contain a great deal of lime, and quickly absorb both water and grease. That is what makes them so suitable. Most of them come from Germany (Solnhofen) and Canada. There are blue and liver-coloured stones. The blue ones are harder and excellent for very fine line work. New stones are expensive and difficult to come by. Beginners should work with used ones. The stone is none the worse for this, but the old drawing must be ground off. It makes a great difference whether it is a week or several years old. The longer a lithographic stone has lain with printing ink on it, the deeper the oil will have penetrated. Grinding will then take longer. If grease remains in the stone, we shall have trouble later on when we print the new drawing. The greasy parts have a tendency to absorb printing ink; it may be possible to deal with this by expert etching, but sometimes there is little we can do, and it is better to start all over again.

Lithographic printing works have practically ceased to exist. In commercial lithography, the stone has been entirely replaced by offset printing from zinc or aluminium plates. The stones have nearly all been got rid of. Some years ago the author saw in one of the Amsterdam canals two barges containing fragments of lithographic stones; they are also used for floors, etc.— another reason why stone is practically unobtainable.

Grinding the stone

The first thing to do is to grind off the old drawing. This is best done with another, smaller lithographic stone. Rotate the latter, add silver sand and water, and keep on grinding until the old work has completely disappeared. The ink of the old drawing takes only five minutes to remove, but this is only the start, because the grease lies deeper, and it may take an hour of scouring, adding fresh sand all the time, before all the grease has disappeared. Some lithographers use some caustic soda to dissolve the grease; it is better, however, to grind with dry sand when we are dealing with very old stones. We then go to work with the whetstone, specially made for this purpose. If we have none, a piece of flat pumice stone will do. The stone must then be polished with a very fine whetstone or snakestone. It must be sound and smooth for the subsequent treatment.

It is not yet suitable for drawing on with lithographic crayon, but must first be given a uniform surface resembling very fine abrasive paper; it must be grained. For graining, we need a glass disc, fine silver sand, ground flint or carborundum powder. Carborundum powder No. 180 is the best graining material. We scatter some of this on the wet, smooth stone, and we apply the disc with small rotations; the smaller these are, the more beautiful and fine the grain will be.

Before graining, we must know whether we wish to draw with crayon or lithographic drawing ink. For crayon, the grain may be somewhat coarser; for ink, a very finely grained stone is best, and sometimes even a smooth stone is desirable.

The crayon is made of fat, soap and blacking; it is obtainable in different grades from very soft to hard as stone and is numbered 1 to 5. The hardest variety, which may be sharpened to a fine point, has no number, but is called "copal". As the crayon contains fat and soap, it breaks readily when held in the hand. A charcoal holder may be a solution. We know that Daumier always drew with small stumps and kept them for melting down and casting into new sticks.

Lithographic drawing ink is used for wash drawings. The ink may be procured in the solid or liquid state. We rub a piece in a dry saucer, and make it into a paste with water; this will take five to ten minutes, because the ink must saponify, and this does not happen at once. It may also be rubbed with turpentine; it then curdles more capriciously on the damp stone. Liquid ink may be bought ready-made; it keeps well in the bottle. Home-made ink is not so good on the following day, and it is preferable to mix a fresh supply after a day.

Preparing the stone

When we have drawn on the stone with crayon, we can scrape portions of the drawing with a sharp knife. Many lithographers use these; a scraper-board knife is also satisfactory. We may draw over these portions with crayon, so that all kinds of textures are formed.

When we print from the stone, the crayon must come off, and the printing ink must replace it. To achieve this and produce not one but several prints, the stone must be treated, or prepared. This treatment decides whether we can print a good edition. We need gum arabic and nitric acid. To prepare the stone properly, do the following well, and you may be sure that printing will raise no difficulties.

1. Rub some fine resin powder carefully over the crayon or ink drawing, and remove the surplus resin powder with talcum powder. The latter forms a smooth layer on the crayon, which is important: the gum etch slides off the fine crayon particles.

2. Rub a layer of gum etch over the stone with a sponge. Gum etch is gum arabic with a few drops of nitric acid (about half a teaspoonful of nitric acid to one cup of dissolved gum). We try out the gum etch first just beside the drawing to see whether it

is too strong; it must effervesce slightly or be on the point of effervescing. If it is too strong, then the etching of the fine crayon portions may be ruined.

3. Leave this layer of gum for at least 24 hours on the stone.

4. The gum etch must now be removed. It is rinsed off with a sponge thoroughly soaked in water or under the tap. To replace it, pure gum must now be applied to the stone. It must penetrate the pores; no gum can enter where there is water. Therefore:

5. We dry the stone.

6. We apply a thin layer of pure gum to the stone and let it dry again. Both the crayon and the gum must be dissolved in the subsequent treatment.

7. We pour a dash of water and a dash of turpentine or turpentine substitute onto the stone and dissolve the crayon with a soft cloth. If this is not done properly, the whole thing may turn out a failure. If we rub too hard, then we may rub away pieces of the greasy stone under the crayon particles and let in gum; these particles will subsequently take up insufficient printing ink, if any, and will give the print a dull, dead tone. When the crayon is dissolved, the stone must be wiped clean with pure water, and the stone may then be rolled up with proving ink.

8. This must also be done with the necessary care. We start with a stiff ink and a good roller. A rough roller is best for crayon, while a smooth leather roller is better for lithograpic drawing ink. Every time we roll up the stone, the latter must be damped; it must have no dry places, but it must not be too wet. It is preferable to pass a squeezed-out sponge over it several times, rather than put water on the stone. The roller must not take up any moisture.

9. A proof may now be pulled, but it is better to etch the stone again first.

10. Roll up the stone, dry it, and carefully rub in resin powder. The latter forms a protective layer on the proving ink. We remove the surplus resin with talcum powder.

11. Proving ink with resin is more resistant to gum etch than lithographic crayon alone, and so the gum etch may be somewhat stronger.

12. After a few minutes we rinse off the gum etch, dry the stone and put it in the pure gum, after which we leave it to dry.

13. We wash the stone with water and turpentine substitute. When it is almost clean and still damp, we may rub it gently with a rag and a dash of wash-out solution to make the greasy parts still greasier. This is not absolutely essential when the stone is in a good state.

14. The stone may now be rolled up again with proving or lithographic drawing ink for the hand press, and then printed.

Proving ink is very stiff and "never" dries, but the edition can be printed quite well with it. This failure to dry comes in useful if we put the stone on one side after printing; after weeks or even months this ink dissolves straight away if we wish to print from the stone again.

During printing the stone must not be allowed to dry. The oil from the printing ink also penetrates the pores laterally, only a little, of course, but the picture as a whole may still become rather dark. This effect helps the stone to fill in. Few lithographers have not been troubled by this when they were beginners. Ink that is too slack may also make the drawing heavier and heavier and finally fill in altogether. Use stiff ink and the correct pressure, and put a dash of gum arabic in the damping water. Quite a good way of preventing filling in is to put a dash of sour beer in the vessel containing the damping water. If the stone still shows a tendency to fill in, pass quickly over it a roller without much ink on, to remove the surplus ink, roll up once again in the usual way, rubbing the hand carefully over the damp stone, and the drawing will usually come right. Rub away the remainder of the tone with a sponge soaked in weak gum etch, and then carry on with printing in the usual way.

We have described "wet" washing-out here. The stone may

also be washed-out without water in the following way. When we have removed the gum etch (4 and 5) we apply a thin layer of pure gum to the stone. This layer must be made really thin by constantly rubbing the palm over the stone and wiping the hand until the stone is quite dry. We wash the drawing carefully with turpentine and a little wash-out solution; thus no water is used. This is followed by damping and rolling up.

The etching of the lithographic stone has quite a different function to that of intaglio etching. With etching, the acid often bites deep into the material; with lithography, a chemical process of importance to this process takes place on the surface. Lithographic drawing ink and crayon do not differ greatly from each other. The former is usually made of beeswax, mutton fat, soap, shellac and soot. Gum etch consists mainly of gum arabic to which some nitric acid and water are added. We should also be able to use old gum arabic that has become acid of its own accord. The writer has had good results with this, particularly with lithographic drawing ink. Gum arabic contains some compounds of arabic acid. Nearly half of lithographic drawing ink and greasy crayon consist of soap. The latter is a compound of alkali and fatty acid. Through the etching process, the nitric acid converts the fatty acid into lime soap. Lime soap readily accepts grease, combines firmly with the stone and becomes a water-insoluble substance; this is important when printing. If we dissolve a piece of lithographic drawing ink in water and add one or two drops of nitric acid, we see that the at first water-soluble ink changes into a water-insoluble, stiff, almost hard substance. If we put into the gum etch the stone on which we have drawn with ink or crayon, the same thing happens as if we had left it in gum etch for 24 hours. The nitric acid changes the ink or crayon, but the gum arabic also undergoes a change, being converted into gum metarabic by the lime and silica in the stone. This substance is also completely insoluble in water, but accepts moisture and is powerfully ink-repellent. Etching adds two new

Detail of etching; drilled holes in the plate produce white beads in relief on the print

First coffer lithographic press according to Senefelder's design

Tools and materials for the lithographer (1 sponge, 2 ink, 3 coarse whetstone, 4 inking roller, 5 lithographic stone, 6 fine whetstone, 7 scraper, 8 carborundum powder, 9 glass disc, 10 raw gum arabic, 11 nitric acid)

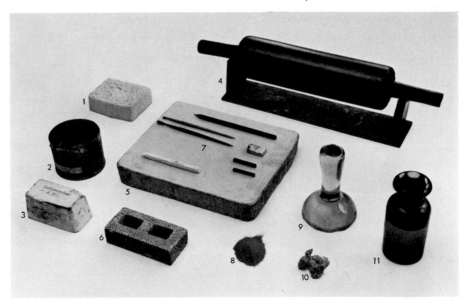

Lithograph (Toulouse Lautrec)

substances; one of these is extra fat-accepting, and the other is extra fat-repellent. This is just what we need for printing.

Printing a stone with an ink drawing on it requires more expert knowledge than when crayon is used. When we draw on a damp stone with ink into which water or turpentine substitute has been rubbed, the ink flows out in capricious forms, and dark tones together with very light-grey ones result. We must retain all these shades in the print. We therefore need to etch and print very carefully. The stone may have to be etched locally with a brush.

There are very many reasons why the printing of a lithograph may end in failure. Incorrect grinding may make the stone rather concave, and this space must be filled up with paper under the tympan. More frequently the stone becomes rather lower on one side owing to incorrect grinding, sometimes by one or two millimetres. We must then lay sheets of paper step-wise under the stone; if we do not do this stepwise the stone may crack under the great pressure. The scraper may have become too blunt through frequent use, or the leather below it may be of variable thickness. Our sponges and cloths may be dirty. The printing ink may be too thin. The tympan must be smooth and everywhere of the same thickness. The damping and neutralizing sponges may be interchanged; this is fatal. It may be too cold or too hot in the workshop. During printing, the stone may be too dry or too wet.

Making corrections on the stone

We may wish to remove a portion of a crayon or ink drawing; it may be ground away with a whetstone or correcting pencil, or a knife may be used. The grain is ground away at the same time, so that it cannot be used again. If we wish to keep the grain, then we may try to dissolve the crayon with petrol, wipe the whole area clean, and remove the grease with a dilute solution of caustic soda. If we have treated the stone with gum, it cannot be drawn on with lithographic crayon. The gum prevents the crayon from adhering to the stone, so that it disappears on damping and rolling up. If we wish to draw on an already prepared stone with ink or crayon, it must be neutralized.

Neutralizing the stone

Chemical treatment is needed to remove the gum arabic. It is so firmly lodged in the pores that it cannot even be rinsed out by pouring water over the stone for days. But it must be eliminated if we wish to add anything on the prepared stone. We neutralize with a saturated solution of alum, but natural vinegar in solution for household use is also quite good. The alum or vinegar is sponged onto the stone, but must not remain for longer than one minute. The stone is then well rinsed to remove any traces of vinegar or alum. When it is dry we can draw on it with crayon or ink wherever necessary. It must then be lightly etched again with gum etch, rinsed, dried and put in pure gum. We have a special sponge for neutralization. If we use it for damping the stone during printing, we shall remove the gum from the pores, and the stone will fill in.

The lithographic press

A lithograph can only be printed on a lithographic press; no other way is possible. When Senefelder invented lithography, a press for printing from the stones did not exist; he made the first prints in the same way as for woodcuts. But this was not very satisfactory, and so he built the first lithographic press. As this looks very like a gallows, we also call it a gallows press. Later, he designed the coffer lithographic press, and later still a press closely resembling the present-day hand press. The stone lies on a kind of carriage moving on rails. The scraper, which is raised and lowered by means of a handle, is in the middle of the press. There are two types of press, with bottom and with top pressure regulator. The best scrapers are made of pear wood. The scraper is about 12 cm (5 in) broad, 2 to 3 cm (1 in) thick and of various lengths. One of the long edges is in the form of a fairly blunt V; a rounded bottom edge is best. A strip of special leather is stretched along this V-shaped edge. When it dries it will be well stretched.

When Senefelder invented the coffer lithographic press, he and many of his contemporaries used one. If this was satisfactory, why did these presses fall out of use? The writer has built one from Senefelder's drawing, and made many prints with it. This kind of press must be very robust; the screw that pulls the scraper over the stone must run on ball-bearings. If the coffer is closed, egg-box closure is best, but it must be made of steel. Other systems may be devised, with the use of key nuts or something similar. Whichever press is used, the scraper and tympan must be well lubricated with grease so that they slide well even under the heaviest pressure.

Lithographic mezzotint

This technique is an old one, which is still used a great deal. The artist starts with a black area, which he scrapes with sharp knives. The stone is well ground so that all the old work is removed. It is best to grind quite smooth, so that no scratches or pits remain. We then provide a fine, uniform grain. The finer and sounder this is the better we shall be able to scrape. If, for example, the stone measures 30 x 40 cm (12 x 16 in) we make a border of thin gum arabic 3 cm (1 in) all round it, so that the lithograph will be 24 x 34 cm (9 x 13 in) since, when it is printed, this border will not accept printing ink. When it is dry we rub the stone evenly with asphalt solution. This asphalt layer dries immediately. We then scrape off the grain here and there with a scraper or sharp knife, exposing the clean stone. Of course many shades may be formed in this way.

Before we start printing, we put the stone in gum arabic and leave it for one or two days. It is then damped and rolled up with stiff proving ink; we must make sure that the scraped parts remain clean and clear. The stone can then be etched in the usual way. It may also now be scraped, or drops of very strong gum etch may be put on it and joined together. The gas bubbles forming in these drops and areas produce a remarkable texture. This procedure is quite personal, of course, and has not got much to do with the actual scraping technique, but that does not prevent a good lithograph from being made in this way.

Lithographic engraving

Lithographic engraving is a quite different technique. It is an obsolete method that was once used for printing letterheads, vouchers and visiting cards, and also for landscapes and portraits.

The stone for a lithographic engraving must be quite smooth. A fine whetstone and snakestone is used. But to make it smooth enough for engraving, we rub the stone well with a rag soaked in dilute sulphuric acid, which converts the top layer of lime into gypsum. The latter fills the finest pores, producing a perfectly mirror-smooth surface. This is coated with a thin layer of gum arabic. When it is dry, the process is repeated, but this time the gum is mixed with some black body colour. When the stone is dry again, the drawing may be engraved with a needle.

Keep the bottom and sides of the groove completely free from gum. In a cold, damp atmosphere the gum is drawn into the fine grooves. And above all, no moist hands! But the great problem is the condensation of the breath while engraving on the stone; to prevent this, we hold a small paper umbrella in the mouth. The stone-engravers of former times also did this. When the

engraving is ready, we rub in some greasy wash-out solution.
When we damp the stone the solution that settles on the gum
arabic disappears, but remains in the grooves, which did not
contain any gum. The stone is now inked like an etching plate
with the dabber, with proving ink mixed with some stiff gum
capable of being kneaded into a ball. The grooves are then filled
with stiff printing ink, and the stone may be etched with gum etch
in the usual way. It is then printed like an etching plate, with
felt on which a zinc tympan is laid. The advantage is that we
print much more quickly and cleanly than from an etching plate,
but aquatints cannot be printed in this way.

Lithographic paper

Lithographic paper is actually a substitute for stone. If we have
not got any handy, it can be bought. There are also many recipes
for making it oneself; an old and good one is as follows:

100 grammes of wheat flour
500 grammes of water
 30 grammes of glycerine
  3 sheets of gelatine
 10 grammes of wood gum
Some yellow poster paint.

Brush the paper with this paste several times in different direc-
tions. A good ready-made starch paste is much simpler and also
quite good; a little glycerine may be added, but this is not necessary. All papers are not suitable for this treatment; the paper
must absorb water readily, and must therefore not be too heavily
sized. Watercolour papers are best. The starch paste must be
spread thinly in three or four coats. When the layer is dry, we
draw on it with lithographic crayon (not lithographic drawing
ink).

The stone on which we print the crayon drawing must be

smooth, and we do not need the grain. It is laid on the lithographic press, neutralized with an alum solution and rinsed well. The crayon drawing is laid on the dry stone after the back of the starch paper has been damped. The stone is then passed through the press. The starch paper must remain on the stone and is now damped again, the press is tightened a little more, and the stone is passed through again. This must be repeated perhaps five or six times with constant damping and tightening. The water must be pressed through the paper on to the layer of starch. The latter is then released. The paper can now be pulled off the stone, which has received the crayon drawing. The remainder of the treatment is as for any crayon drawing.

Colour prints

So far we have only used black ink, but lithography is also an excellent way of producing colour prints. Suppose we wish to print a lithograph in five colours; we need five stones. If we are making a design in colour, we must first decide, as with colour woodcuts, whether we wish to print the colours beside or over each other. We make an outline drawing of all the colours and draw them on a stone with lithographic drawing ink; in the middle of the two ends we put a registration cross, also with lithographic drawing ink, and print this outline drawing off the stone. We coat the still wet print with charcoal powder and print this offset on to the smooth or finely grained stones.

We may also use another method, which is much simpler for our purpose. We draw the outlines on transparent paper with crayon No. 3 and ensure that the lines are as narrow as possible; we do not forget the registration crosses and print the drawing by hand on the stones standing ready. Each stone is allotted its own colour. Although we shall later on be printing in yellow, red or blue, all the stones are marked with black lithographic crayon or drawing ink.

When we have prepared the stone and are going to print, we roll it up with the desired colour. We usually start with the lightest colour, but this is not necessary. After the first print, we cut a corner from the registration cross with a knife, so that this corner fits the cross exactly in the case of the second stone, which we roll up with a different colour.

For larger editions this is very complicated. The writer has printed many editions of two hundred to three hundred in six and eight colours on a hand press, adopting the following procedure. The sheets of paper must all be square and of the same size. When a sheet has passed eight times under the press, it becomes somewhat damp; it has stretched 1 or 2 mm after the eighth printing. Exact fits are then impossible. Therefore, pull the paper once through the press, and most of its stretch will be taken out. Or hang up ten sheets together. When paper hangs for some days it becomes longer. These two methods are often used in lithographic printing works.

Instead of using crosses, we may adopt the following procedure. The offset must be just as square and of the same size as the sheets to be printed. We put a corner on the stone with lithographic drawing ink and, at the same level, a line; both the offset and paper must fit in here exactly.

Every artist will use his own method for printing colour lithographs. One will want greasy, shiny prints, in which the colours do not fit so exactly. Another will want dull colours printed thinly over each other, and this also gives good results. It is best to print a colour when the previous one is dry. After three or four printings the paper is sometimes saturated and no longer absorbs oil from the printing ink, so that it will become shiny. To prevent this we may coat thinly with magnesium powder when the previous printing is almost dry; this will make the paper absorb the next application of ink better, so that it will not be shiny.

If you print editions in many colours for years, you may

achieve remarkable effects. The writer once printed a number of colour lithographs for which he started with a very thin, distinctly visible and quite even tone of grey; he had also used a scraper. He gave the stone a rolling up with sparingly applied black printing ink and applied some pressure on printing. At each successive printing he applied rather more pressure, so that he was able to print ten times with a single rolling up, and no difference was visible between the ten prints. This naturally requires some skill.

The colour-fastness of the printing ink is very important. Cheap inks are not light-fast, and they also contain fillers, so that the particles of pigment are much further away from each other with diluted than with undiluted inks. The writer has carried out tests with inks; the prints lay for some time under mercury lamps, sometimes producing disappointing results and sometimes good ones, showing no deterioration.

Finally it must be said that the techniques to which all these pages are devoted are only an aid. What matters is what we do with them. When we look at prints, we may dwell on them for a moment, but we must forget the technique as soon as possible, because quite different values are involved in graphic art.

Other materials used in lithography

Stone is the best material; a thick one may last you practically all your life. If stones have become too thin after years of use, they can quite easily be cemented together. Corrections are much more satisfactory than on other materials; a stone can be scraped and scratched.

But this does not alter the fact that quite good results can be achieved on plates of zinc and aluminium. The zinc plates that are used in offset printing are obtainable grained. But we can grain them for ourselves with carborundum powder No. 180. We use a glass disc and water to grain the surface of the zinc or aluminium plate. It must be completely flat; we therefore lay it on a moist sheet of glass, when it will not slip away.

After graining, we neutralize the zinc plate with a saturated alum solution or a 4 per cent acetic acid solution. We can then draw on it with lithographic crayon or drawing ink. The composition of gum etch for zinc plates is quite different to that of the gum etch used for printing with stone. Gum etch is made with the following ingredients:

    10 grammes of ammonium phosphate
    10 grammes of ammonium nitrate
1000 grammes of gum arabic dissolved in water.

We pour a dash of this gum etch on the zinc plate, which we rub with the hand until dry; this is followed by washing-out with turpentine and wash-out solution. Next, the plate is rinsed under flowing water. It can then be rolled up and printed from.

If a portion of the drawing has to be removed, it can be ground away with a correcting pencil dipped in soda. It is difficult to add anything; this can only be done with a silver or copper pencil. The areas are inked with the finger, damped and rolled up. The surplus printing ink is removed by rolling up. If we wish to make a new drawing on an already printed zinc or aluminium plate, we may clean it entirely with a brush and a solution of caustic soda. Neutralize, and the plate is ready for another drawing. But the grain must not have been damaged too much by correcting pencils. Aluminium plates are first neutralized with an alum solution or a solution of 40 grammes of oxalic acid to 960 grammes of water. A brush is used. The plate may then be drawn on with crayon or ink and etched, like the zinc plate, but with a different gum etch:

600 grammes of gum arabic
  10 grammes of phosphoric acid.

Then roll up and print.

By the end of the last war, practically no material was obtainable for lithography, particularly gum arabic. We know the chemical action of gum arabic on stone; it is therefore surprising to learn that a lithographic gum of quite a different composition has the same action. One graphic school made up a lithographic gum consisting practically entirely of dextrin. The writer liked this so much that he continued to use it for years after the war. The same applies to turpentine and turpentine substitute; the writer used petroleum with the same result.

When printing etchings and lithographs, especially etchings, our hands often get very dirty; there are many agents for cleaning them. First rub chalk powder well into the hands so that the pores are filled. After work, green soap with fresh coffee grounds is best.

Black spirit varnish may often stick obstinately after the fixing of the aquatint when the etching plate is cleaned. In such cases, use a mixture of thinner and spirit. If it will not dissolve, then use a varnish-remover; this will not attack the plate.

SILK-SCREEN PRINTING

This process has existed for a long time, and it has been and is practised a great deal in Japan, but it is still very young in Europe. Nevertheless, in a few dozen years it has made great strides. It is used mainly for advertising, particularly in textile-printing works. It has the great advantage that it is very suitable for printing on cardboard, wood, glass, etc. A number of artists, both painters and draughtsmen, have used the technique and achieved very good results.

As the name implies, silk-screen printing is based on the screening of the printing ink. The screen consists of a frame made of wood and metal on which silk or nylon is stretched. When this is laid on paper and the ink is pressed through the screen with a strip of rubber, known as the squeegee, we have a uniformly printed surface. If we cover part of the silk with a liquid, so that its meshes are filled and the liquid dries, and if we then press the ink through the meshes with the squeegee, then only the open meshes will let it through. This is the principle of silk-screen printing.

In a silk-screen works, the drawing or the text is usually applied to the screen by photographic means, photosensitive preparations being used. Artists may, of course, also avail themselves of this quite new printing method, and some of them do.

This technique may be used without photographic aids, such as negatives, lamps and photosensitive layers. For example, we may draw with a brush directly on the stretched surface, that is to say fill the meshes with a liquid, for example cellulose lacquer, whereupon these lines and surfaces will not let any ink through, or we may draw with greasy lithographic crayon. We are then using the principle that any places drawn on with crayon will subsequently let ink through. This sounds strange, but will immediately become clear. The meshes must be filled really well with the crayon; it is best to draw on the back of the drawing with the same crayon, so that they are well filled on both sides. When this has been done, we pour a strip of cellulose lacquer quickly on to one end of the frame and spread it all over the screen with the squeegee, which usually has a wooden handle. All the meshes are filled, except where we have drawn with lithographic crayon. When the lacquer is dry, we can dissolve the crayon with turpentine on the back, where the lacquer has not been applied to it. We then see that the whole crayon drawing appears to us in open meshes.

Anyone who wishes to use this technique will, of course, have to carry out various other operations, which cannot be dealt with in this book in a couple of pages. There are many manuals and technical journals telling us everything about silk-screen printing. But we did not wish to omit all reference to it in this little book.

EXPERIMENTATION

EVERY now and again we see in history people who try out something new. If the time is not yet ripe for their experiments they continue to toil away on their own, as Hercules Seghers did. The new abstract trend in graphic art is forcing the artist constantly to use new techniques. Many experiments come to nothing; that is not such a bad thing. If some of their inextinguishable urge to seek and try out has results, then the artists round them or those that come after may well benefit.

Sometimes, artists have no interest at all in the experiments of their contemporaries. Take Hercules Seghers in the first half of the seventeenth century. He was interested first and foremost in printing. Whereas most etchers say after printing, "That's that", this was only the beginning for Seghers. Everyone knows that we can take another impression on clean paper from a fresh print; we then get a counter-impression, which is at the expense of the first impression, and the second one is of poorer quality. But Seghers probably printed a first impression on a new polished plate, touched up the counter-impression, scattered some resin powder, on it, warmed the plate, stopped-out here and there, and then etched the plate in different states. The result has the very mysterious effect of some of his prints. It is not certain that he used this technique, but it seems probable in some etchings.

Seghers also sometimes printed on previously toned paper and linen, and with white ink on black paper. He very probably used a kind of soft-ground technique. Recent investigations suggest strongly that he was the first to use aquatint; he also employed a kind of sugar-aquatint technique. This artist continued to experiment intensively and certainly used unknown methods, which we can only guess at.

A similar figure was the timber-merchant, collector and etcher, Ploos van Amstel. Although not a great artist, he experimented with etching plates in every possible way, an important part being played by sand and iron filings. He was searching in particular for a method of imitating a crayon line in the etching technique.

Other examples may be mentioned in the history of graphic art. But it is in our own times above all that this is being practised intensively, particularly by the young graphic artists who feel strongly drawn towards etching, so that experimentation is now a centre of interest.

The fascination of wonderful textures has triggered off all this experimenting on etching plates. Taboos no longer exist; everything is permitted if it benefits expression. Black spirit varnish is used to stop-out the back of the plate. It is hard; if we scratch it with a needle it crumbles off the plate, especially where the lines intersect. What we try to avoid with a good etching ground is deliberately caused in order to obtain this frayed line. Others scratch this hard layer with knives; resin is scattered on it, and deep-bitten aquatints produce coarse structures in capricious forms. The same effect can be achieved by dissolving asphalt powder in petrol (warm on a water bath). We can subsequently scrape and scratch this solution when it has been brushed on and dried.

When we apply resin powder by means of an aquatint box or screen, we must not jolt the plate before the resin particles have been fixed, or they will roll about. Nevertheless, the writer has given the side edge of a plate dusted in this way a sharp tap with a hammer to give the resin grains a "start". Capricious aquatint forms result when we heat the plate, etch and, if we wish, dust once again.

An etcher should see that his plate does not oxidize if he wants it to keep, but the artist sometimes wishes to have severely oxidized areas. The zinc plate is then treated with strong chlorine water and vinegar and for a few days with fresh chlorine water now and again; very severely oxidized parts are then formed, which may give surprising results on printing.

Instead of using needles, we may draw in the normal ground with a hard pencil; the lines will then be different. If these narrow lines, and especially the broad lines as well, are etched and we wish to print jet black, aquatint must be applied in the lines. We lay a ground, so that it does not enter the lines, using a hard rubber roller. The plate is then put in the aquatint box and warmed, so that the resin or asphalt powder melts. This is followed by etching, when the lines have an aquatint and will hold the ink better.

To get capricious, deeply impressed textures, some artists use the soldering iron. The finest solder lines can be obtained with some practice. They are flattened a little at the first printing, but after that they keep their shape. Copper wires soldered on to the etching plate and small, thin pieces of metal, such as parts from watches, give wonderful effects on printing when the plate has been well wiped. Drilling large and small holes into the plate also produces an interesting effect. Ink cannot enter these holes. On printing, the felt will press the paper into the holes so that white beads appear on the etching.

Modern apparatus is being used more and more in graphic art. Young graphic artists, among them A. van Kerkhoven, searching for methods of forming new textures on the etching plate, have started using oxyacetylene and electric welders. There would naturally be no sense in using such methods if the result could be achieved by much simpler means.

The surface of the zinc or copper can be made to flow with an oxyacetylene welder. The resulting texture is reminiscent of the patterns traced by Jack Frost on the windows in winter. But beware of the very dangerous gases.

Propane gas is easier to use and has the same results. A second method of forming different textures is to use an electric welder, when the arc plays an important part. The latter generates so much heat that the underlying metal melts and small craters are formed. The metal that is flung off sticks to the plate. The action of the arc can be regulated by raising or lowering the current strength. Here too the vapours are poisonous, and a helmet should be worn.

Surprising results may also be achieved, of course, by many less spectacular methods according to the fancy and inventiveness of the artist.

The writer once needed black and white drops of different sizes in an etching. The zinc plate was $1\frac{1}{2}$ mm thick. The ground was rolled onto the plate, small and large drops of petrol were dropped onto it with a good brush (turpentine substitute may also be used), and the drops were carefully absorbed by blotting paper (filter paper will do). The plate was then etched long and deep, and the etched drops were given a fine asphalt aquatint in the usual way. The writer wished to have one or two white drops scattered among all those black ones, and so he simply drilled large and small holes in the plate. To print sound edges, he filed the drilled holes smooth with a rat-tailed file.

One may well ask whether all this messing about with an etching plate is really necessary. No, it is not necessary; the most beautiful results can be achieved simply with a bitten line etching in all styles from the most naturalistic to the most abstract that can be imagined. But if nobody ever wanted to try something different we should still be in the Stone Age. And that goes for graphic art as well.

Experiment; various metal objects soldered to the plate

Treating a zinc plate with a welding burner

Detail of a treated plate

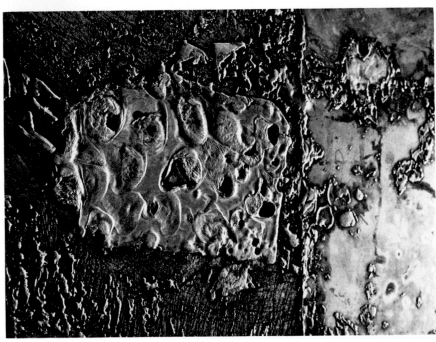

Treating with a welding electrode

Detail of a plate

Result of treating a zinc plate with an electrode welder, with a print (white ink on black paper)

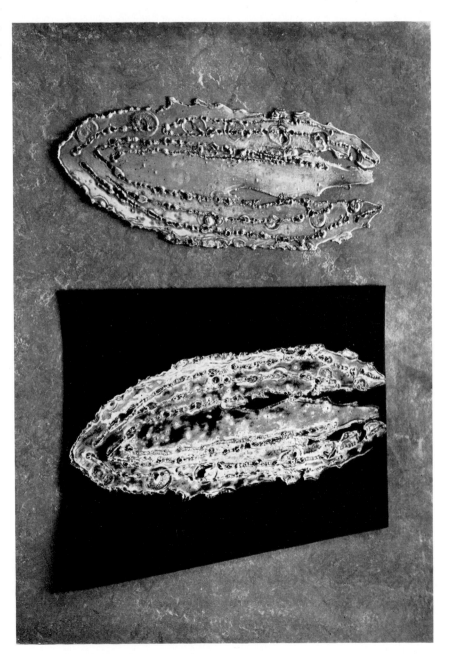